Moshoeshoe e Moholo 1786 - 1870
(Moshoeshoe the Great)

THE MEMOIRS OF SPENCER "TED" NETTELTON

WORKING IN THE COLONIAL SERVICE IN LESOTHO

The Memoirs of Spencer "Ted" Nettelton:
Working in the Colonial Service in Lesotho

ISBN 978-0-6486506-1-4

© Spencer Enraght "Ted" Nettelton, 2018
First published 2018

All rights reserved. Without limiting the rights under copyright reserved above, no part of this publication may be reproduced, stored in or introduced into a database and retrieval system or transmitted in any form or any means (electronic, mechanical, photocopying, recording or otherwise) without the prior written permission of the author or authorised representative.
Contact Beverley Eikli at beverley.writer@gmail.com

Original photographs by Spencer Enraght "Ted" Nettelton

ALSO BY SPENCER 'TED' NETTELTON

The Memoirs of Spencer "Ted" Nettelton:
Growing up in Botswana in the 1930s and 40s

The Memoirs of Spencer Enraght Nettelton:
My Career in Australia

The Diaries of Gerald Nettelton

Nettelton Family History

The Memoirs of Clement Geoffrey Nettelton OBE, 1893–1986
From South Africa to the world — and back home

Contents

Preface • 1

King Moshoeshoe • 4

Black-White Relationships Day to Day in the Colonial Era in Lesotho and Bechuanaland • 5

A Snapshot of My Life in Maseru in the Mid-1950s • 8

Court at Marakabei • 12

Private Secretary to Sir John Maud • 34

What Did a District Commissioner Do? • 49

A Few Initiatives in Mokhotlong District • 56

In Power • 60

Lesotho 1960 — International Politics in a Changing World • 66

On Trek in the Mountains of Lesotho • 68

Recollections of the Sani Pass in the 1950s and 60s • 74

First Date with Gail – 1959 • 88

Gail Franklin Nettelton (nee Turner) • 89

Life in British Colonial Days • 101

Trout Fishing in Lesotho • 110

Stephen Phakisi • 118

Air Travel in Basutoland • 120

Food for Work • 126

Food and Fodder Relief • 131

The Diamonds of Letseng la Terae • 134

Mokhotlong Roads in the 1960s • 142

Mokhotlong Fun and Recreation • 147

Mokhotlong Traditional Scenes, Early 1960s • **156**

Chief Leabua Jonathan • **160**

Politics between Lesotho and South Africa in the Lead-up to Lesotho Independence and just after (1961-1966) • **165**

Lesotho Independence Celebrations • **168**

Political Controversies Before and After Lesotho Independence 1966 • **184**

A Visit to the United States • **199**

A Visit to Malawi • **214**

Chief Leabua's Coup • **219**

Mixing with Royalty • **228**

All the World's a Stage • **230**

Family Tragedies • **232**

Queen's Birthday Honours Disappointment • **234**

Departure for Australia • **235**

Mountain village

Preface

After reading my memoirs, I hope you will better understand, as politically incorrect it may seem to be in modern times, why I remain an unapologetic product of the British Colonial Empire, as was Rudyard Kipling, well-known author of the late Victorian-era poem 'If'.

IF

If you can keep your head when all about you
Are losing theirs and blaming it on you,
If you can trust yourself when all men doubt you,
But make allowances for their doubting too;
If you can wait and not be tired by waiting,
Or being lied about, don't deal in lies,
Or being hated, don't give way to hating,
And yet don't look too good, nor talk too wise:

If you can dream—and not make dreams your master;
If you can think—and not make thoughts your aim;
If you can meet with Triumph and Disaster
And treat those two impostors just the same;
If you can bear to hear the truth you've spoken
Twisted by knaves to make a trap for fools,
Or watch the thing you gave your life to, broken,
And stoop and build 'em up with worn-out tools:

If you can make one heap of all your winnings
And risk it on one turn of pitch-and-toss
And lose, and start again at your beginnings
And never breathe a word about your loss;
If you can force your heart and nerve and sinew
To serve your turn long after they are gone,
And so hold on when there is nothing in you
Except the Will who says to them "Hold on!"

If you can talk with crowds and keep your virtue,
Or walk with kings—nor lose the common touch,
If neither foes nor loving friends can hurt you,
If all men count with you, but none too much;
If you can fill the unforgiving minute
With sixty seconds' worth of distance run,
Yours is the earth and everything that's in it,
And—which is more—you'll be a Man, my son!

By Rudyard Kipling. First published 1910

I have enjoyed the writings of Rudyard Kipling who epitomised the spirit of colonialist Britain when at the zenith of its power. I unashamedly admit that I am proud to have been a member of the British administrative structure which governed so many British colonies spread around the world, and in our family heritage there are so many others who, like me, were very much involved in British Colonial issues whether these were military, government administration or private commercial enterprise.

Kipling's verse 'If ' portrays to me the image of an adventurous, brave and honourable man of that era and I would have been proud to be likened to such a man. It would be fashionable in our modern era to demonise him as a white "colonialist oppressor". I was there and I never felt like an oppressor. I left the British Colonial Service with no feelings of guilt, rather with pride, because we left behind a system of administration, which functioned.

I believe judgment of our British rule should be made on the basis of whether or not the ordinary man in the street is better off now than they were in colonial days, not solely on the basis of the political freedom of the elite few to make decisions for the running of the country and control of its economy which all too often entails maximising their own wealth and privilege with little regard for ordinary citizens. This is not the case in many countries but any fair-minded person would have to concede that this is nevertheless a widespread problem.

The hostility towards the British Empire is particularly orchestrated by a group of journalists, historians and film makers who accentuate those issues and events which were not to the credit of the Empire (and in every history of every nation there will always be good and bad) but say little or nothing about the good things that were achieved. I strongly contend that much of that which has been written is not fairly balanced. And I further contend that the views of the ordinary citizen of a newly independent state should not be sought in the early days of nationalistic fervour but a decade or so down the track when the reality of "freedom from the British yoke" can be more accurately gauged as against the quality of life under a new regime of independence. And those views should be ascertained not just from the upper echelon of the community but also from the ordinary person in the street.

After browsing through this volume of my memoirs I hope you will feel able to conclude that although I am a British Empire loyalist, I was never a heartless exploiter of the people I helped to administer.

As stated in an earlier volume of my memoirs, my principal objective has been to record the detail of the day by day life of a District Commissioner both at work and socially in the British Colonial era in Africa which spanned one hundred years from 1880 to 1980. That era has now gone and will never be repeated.

King Moshoeshoe I of Lesotho (1786-1870)

Moshoeshoe I was the founder of the Basutho nation. Before Moshoeshoe took control the Basuto were a scattered people in small villages and therefore very vulnerable to attack from the powerful and aggressive Zulus who stole their cattle, kidnapped their women and burnt their villages. Also the Boers from the south were already encroaching on their fertile land in what became the Orange Free State. Moshoeshoe persuaded these villages to amalgamate as a single unit thus far better able to ward off attacks from the Zulus and Boers.

His political acumen in reading the political realities of the era was uncanny: he sought and gained British protection and Lesotho became a British colony.

He invited the Paris Evangelical Mission to Lesotho and stipulated that they could build their churches and schools but they would never own the land they built on. He banned witchcraft, the import of European liquor and lobola (bride price).

Moshoeshoe was one of those outstanding men who would stand on their own as a great man in any society. He was a man of peace and respected by all citizens of his era both black and white. The world as I write in 2019 could do with a few politicians with his qualities.

Black-White Relationships Day to Day in the Colonial Era in Lesotho and Bechuanaland

An issue to which I have not devoted much attention in this memoir is that of the relationship towards one another of the black and white populations: in my case, between the non-white Basuto on one side and us, the Colonial interlopers, on the other.

I can honestly say that there was a high degree of respect on both sides but at official level in the public service, and the managerial level in the wider community, there was an acceptance that the white segment of the community held the reins of authority. In Lesotho, it was not until the mid-1950s that a challenge to that state of affairs began to evolve. The challenge came mainly from the ranks of the well-educated Basotho entering the political arena and they quite understandably resented their subservience to the white community within their own country.

The issue was given greater traction by the growing interest in Africa of both Russia and China who were increasingly seeking to augment their own respective interests all over the world. The wealth of raw materials that Africa still had in abundance and which had not as yet been exploited was very attractive. But in achieving this goal it was also important to get them to accept communism as the best way forward. Often this entailed blatant bribery with the African leaders well paid personally (like Mugabe). The money went to political parties sympathetic to either Russia or China, not to projects.

By 1959 when I was appointed District Commissioner Maseru, the financial support of potentially subversive Basuto political parties was considerable. This posed a great threat to Lesotho in that South Africa, still in the apartheid era and almost paranoid about communism, would not have tolerated even a low level of subversion generated by a political group which used the protection of a foreign country to avoid retribution after committing an act of sabotage in South Africa then slipping across the border—the Caledon river—into Lesotho where they were safe.

I have written elsewhere as to what I regard as the great contribution Chief Leabua Jonathan made towards the maintenance of a cordial relationship with South Africa despite the hostility to his approach by many Basuto elements within Lesotho and just about every non-white country which held a safe seat in the United Nations General Assembly.

Leabua defied the odds opposing him and successfully walked a tightrope between retaining good relations with South Africa but also demonstrating that he was not a puppet of South Africa.

But to return to black-white relations in Lesotho. I believe an important element of the harmony goes way back to 1880 when Lord Lugard drew up a framework in which newly acquired land in Africa would be administered. This policy sought to build upon existing cultural structures of authority and not to break them down. The outcome of this was that at lower levels the village headmen and most chiefs found their day-to-day authority was not taken away from them. Even the senior chiefs still had status and influence but it all had to happen within a legal and broader administrative structure as determined by Britain. The result was that the policy was not overly destructive.

In Lesotho, there was not much social intermixing. At official functions the Basuto men who attended seldom brought their wives. In the early 1960s with independence looming, wives started to come to functions. At first it was obviously quite stressful for most such wives but over a period of a few years this steadily worked itself out. Some wives were happy to simply stay at home and this was taken by all as quite acceptable. The confidence of other wives increased when they came to functions and obviously enjoyed them.

At page 86 I have written about issues that occurred when hotels in their front bars and lounges became open to Basuto (the restrictions on access to European alcohol were imposed initially in the 19th century by King Moshoeshoe I) and I believe this factor had a bearing on the slowness of the introduction of laws allowing Basuto free access to alcohol.

The story at page 103-04 about two Afrikaners from apartheid South Africa in the early 1960s who found themselves in the same golf foursome as a black player at an intertown competition is both amusing and groundbreaking. Dr A.D. Lebona, an African doctor working in Lesotho, handled the situation brilliantly. Those two white Afrikaners ended up admitting afterwards that this African was a good chap. This is an illustration of how the relationship between black and white was starting to ease.

The basis of my own approach was that I saw no merit in trying to push myself into an artificial social situation. I respected every Mosotho* as a person and I hope they looked at me in the same manner. For the most part Gail and I socialised in the white portion of Lesotho society but there were many occasions during which Basotho came to a social situation at our house or stayed with us, particularly in Mokhotlong. The Basotho involved were mainly well educated and comfortable with the situation.

I have written elsewhere about the many visits Chief Matlere who spoke no English paid to our house at his own volition and we used to talk through an interpreter very freely and in a very friendly manner. The mutual friendship which existed between Chief Leabua and myself was another illustration of a good relationship but conducted in a manner in which both of us felt comfortable.

*Mosotho – a person of the Basotho ethnic group; citizen of Lesotho (plural: Basuto)

A Snapshot of My Life in Maseru in the Mid-1950s

On my return from Cambridge in 1955 I settled well into my new position in the District Office in Maseru. Peter Hughes gave me a great deal of latitude in the work I did. Many years later, when I asked why he had been so lenient in his attitude to me, he said, "Well, there were two things. One, I felt you could do the job, and the other was because I was so bloody lazy by that stage in my career."

Life in Maseru was very pleasant. I played a lot of cricket and over the next couple of years made a lot of runs and took a lot of wickets, and thoroughly enjoyed it all. I also played a lot of golf, won a few mugs and brought my handicap down to twelve. There was always company and someone with whom to play a game of golf, or go trout fishing, bass fishing or do a bit of guinea fowl shooting. I had my reliable Vauxhall sedan and Dennis Hobson was still around. He drove an MG sports car which stood up to the rough roads extremely well. Dennis was always good company; I missed Rupert who was still somewhere overseas. Liz Tennant was around but by that stage she was engaged to a guy from Scotland.

Lesotho Cricket XI, 1956. I am third from right.

Despite this we remained good friends and saw a lot of one another. Ann Duncan had returned from overseas and it was good to have her in our social group. I saw quite a lot of her. There was always good company and lots to do and I enjoyed the work.

My family were not at all musical and not interested in the arts whereas the group of friends I had in Maseru (Ann, Dennis, Rupert) were passionate about these things. I owe them a great debt because they taught me so much and ultimately I was as passionate as they were and I became quite knowledgeable.

What About Official Duties?

It was still the time of the Raj and a very privileged time for the white Colonialist, but we were just entering the fringes of a political era. As a District Officer my own feelings at that time leant towards a fairly conservative approach which strongly backed the maintenance of the hereditary chief system and I felt myself rather hostile towards the up and coming disrespectful and questioning politicians. Russia and China during this era were both interested in expansion of their areas of infuence and a trickle of money had already started coming in to support African political parties that sought to overthrow British Colonial control. This trickle grew to a flood over the next four to six years. In Lesotho, the Russians poured money into the Africa National Congress led by a university graduate known as Ntsu Mokhehle and the Chinese supported a different party known as Marema-Tlou, led by a university graduate who had an extremely good intellect.

View of Maseru town with the hospital in the foreground. The hills in the background are across the Caledon River.

Thatch was extensively used. This is the cultural centre in Maseru.

About 1958 a full-time magistrate was appointed in Maseru so I no longer had to do court work. This was a great relief because in 1960 I was appointed as the fully fledged District Commissioner, Maseru. I had five District Chiefs to deal with and a volatile political situation. I was greatly assisted by the fact that I had known most of the important political leaders from previous years and we still seemed able to talk to one another and respect one another. The Special Branch told me that I was number two on the Basutoland Congress Party hit list (Ken Shortt-Smith, senior police officer for the Maseru District, was number one), but that never worried me. I continued to have good relations with the senior political party members. The role of the District Commissioner had in the space of a couple of years changed dramatically. I still enjoyed the work.

Matters of the Heart

I guess I was a reasonably eligible bachelor in that era. Certainly I was invited to many parties, both dinner and cocktail. I knew a lot of people and as a District Officer I had status on the top rung of the Government structure. One thing saddened me and that was that it was becoming more and more obvious that my relationship with Morag had no future. A year down the track, her parents were still opposing her coming out to Lesotho. We wrote long letters to one another but she ultimately formed a romantic relationship with a doctor whom she married quite a number of years later, and they went to live in Leeds. I saw her for a few days on my next visit

Maseru Post Office.
In the late 1950s the Department of Posts and Telegraphs had a tight budget. To save money stamps had no adhesive on the reverse side. In the corner of each post office was a pot of glue and one pasted each stamp on to the envelope before posting it.

Maseru Roman Catholic Cathedral — a fine sandstone building. 'Penance labour' helped build many a Roman Catholic facility in Lesotho.

to the UK in late 1959 but by that stage her relationship with the doctor was well established.

We remained friends, but probably it was a good thing that we ultimately lost touch. During that time in Lesotho, that is from 1954 to 1958, I never formed any strong and lasting relationship although I frequently went out with girls. I enjoyed their company and had a good time but there was nothing serious between me and any girl, but in 1959 Liz Tennant and I, who had known one another for a long time, started a serious relationship and we would probably have married had I not at that time been appointed as Private Secretary to the British High Commissioner which meant moving away from Lesotho. The tyranny of distance came into play and I met and ultimately married Gail and Liz married Captain Ken Shortt-Smith. Location and timing play an important part in determining who you marry. I was twenty-nine and I guess Gail and I met at the right time. Over the next thirty-five years of marriage I never had any regrets.

Court at Marakabei
Experiences as a young District Officer, 1954–56

Road across the lowland plain looking towards the mountains.

Dispensing Justice in the Mountains

On my return from Cambridge in early 1955, I was required to pass both my law and language examinations. These were set by the Service and I was given two years in which to pass all exams otherwise my pay increments would be held back. I was required to do criminal law, civil law and statutory law at the level required and there was a hell of a lot of work involved. My time at Cambridge was a great asset to me because we had concentrated so much on criminal law. As a District Officer I had jurisdiction in court up to one year's imprisonment or $100 fine. After passing my law exams, which I soon did, my jurisdiction was increased to two years' imprisonment or $200 fine.

Once a month I drove up to Marakabei to do a court session which lasted about three days. My court cases were almost entirely made up

Marakabei Police post, a two-room stone and thatch building. This is where I conducted a three-day court session once a month.

of assaults and stock theft. There was a small Police post at Marakabei and I dealt with the cases that arose from that area.

Lesotho consists of a lowland plain on the western side and on the east, the very mountainous area. The plain takes up about one third of the country and the rest is the mountains. In the mid-1950s there were few roads into the mountains. The Mountain road, as we called it, to Marakabei was the first big road engineering project undertaken in Lesotho and this road penetrated about a hundred kilometres towards the centre of the mountain area.

The trip from Maseru to Marakabei took about three hours, all on dirt road. I travelled in a four-wheel-drive vehicle and took staff with me consisting of an interpreter and a political messenger. At Marakabei the Police were responsible for preparing the detail of everything before the matter came to my court. The Police post was headed by an African Police Corporal with about six Police Troopers. They had no motor vehicle at their disposal; all their work was done on horseback.

The Police Station consisted of a two-room building constructed from local stone with a thatched roof. When conducting court I normally sat outside in the sun wearing my hat and sunglasses and it could get really hot. The Police Corporal did the prosecution and the interpreter sat alongside me and did all the interpretation. Every word of evidence had to be written down in longhand by me. It was a long and laborious process but at least one could be satisfied that everyone understood what was being said and hopefully what was going on. Any accused found guilty and sentenced to a term of imprisonment had to go down to the jail in Maseru. The Police had a rather crackly radio communication with the District Police Office in Maseru and they would make arrangements for a vehicle to be sent up to take the prisoners down.

Assault cases arose mainly from altercations at beer-drinking parties. The traditional drink in Lesotho at that time was joala which was a heavy beer made from ground sorghum. I found joala most unpalatable but the local population loved it and it in fact was a healthy drink, unless taken in very large quantities, because it contained a high Vitamin B content.

Parties were often arranged to encourage people to come to the Australian equivalent of a working bee at harvesting or weeding time. The owner of the land would provide the beer and everyone was welcome to come along and participate so long as they did their share of work. I'm sure there were many shirkers and quarrels obviously did arise, no doubt inflamed by excess alcohol, and fights took place. There were also

Mountain man with horse and foal. The blanket is traditional with much variation in colour and design. In a cold climate the blanket substitutes for an overcoat.

some cases of husbands assaulting their wives and another man was frequently involved. In the Marakabei area assault was a problem and I was quite severe on persons who I found guilty.

The mountains of Lesotho are essentially sheep and angora goat country, with a few cattle. The land is all communally owned with no fences. There are traditional boundaries between various areas so if you were a citizen under Chief A, you would generally be expected to keep out of the territory of Chief B. These boundaries were not well defined and were often in dispute. Because there were no fences, stock theft was a lot easier and animals could be taken during the night and by daylight be a long way away and difficult to find, bearing in mind the mountainous terrain. Every person was entitled to register an ear mark. This mark was cut into the ear of the animal and a stock thief would normally endeavour to obliterate the ear mark by cutting away a piece of the ear then adding their own ear mark. As Magistrate, one was always extremely suspicious of an animal brought before the court as an exhibit which had chunks cut out of its ears and a new ear mark cut in. When a flock of sheep or goats were brought before the court with the allegation that they had been stolen by an accused, one depended on ear marks and also identification by the allegedly true owner of his own animals plus any other corroborating witnesses.

Looking back on those days in court I realise that the Police did not have an easy job with no roads in place. When a case was coming before the court they had to go out on horseback to serve summonses and bring exhibits in, or keep the exhibits in the Police Pound until the case came up. There was no question of jumping into a vehicle and serving a summons on someone living in such and such a street or getting them on the telephone, let alone on their mobile phone or putting a fax or email through to them. At times the weather was very inclement and one has to respect those policemen who had to go out on their horses over mountain trails, riding for many hours to ensure that everything was done to enable the court to function properly.

Police trooper on patrol.

Typical mountain shepherd scene. Youngsters often looked after the flocks in remote areas without adult daily supervision.

Rugged mountain country through which police had to ride to deal with investigations.

The Government Resthouse — Hundreds of Red-Eyed Spiders

When staying at Marakabei I lived at the Government Resthouse on the Mantsonyane River about three miles from the Police Station. The river ran all year round and it was a pleasant setting apart from the fact that the roof of the Resthouse, which was made of reeds and thatch, was the place of residence of hundreds of spiders. They only came out at night once the lights were out. If you woke up in the middle of the night and shone your torch on the thatched roof above you, you caught the reflection of dozens of eyes in the torch glow. It was very disconcerting having all those spiders crawling around above and you wondered whether the time would come when the odd one would lose its grip and drop on you. I got used to it and slept well and I was not aware of any that fell on me. At least they confined themselves to the roof and didn't seem to come down on to the floor or the furniture.

Irish Politics in the Mountains

Marakabei did not have much of a resident population. Europeans were the shopkeeper and two Roman Catholic priests. The trading stall belonged to the big trading conglomerate, Frasers. The shop was managed by an Irish Protestant called Bob Morrison. He was a bachelor who was always immaculate in his dress and never went without shaving. He had a nicely fitted out house and was respected by the Africans. His shop served the surrounding community, not only in terms of food, clothing, household goods, etc for purchase but the shop also bought wool, mohair, cattle and any excess grain that people might have for sale. A bit of mountain wheat was grown in the valleys. The shop would have done very well. The income of the population was always much enhanced by money remitted home by men working contracts in the South African gold and diamond mines.

Bob Morrison had an ongoing feud with the Roman Catholic Mission. It was all very Irish—Catholic versus Protestant—way out in these mountains of Lesotho. There was an occasion when one of the local brothers from the Catholic Mission came before me in court for reckless driving. He had come round a corner a bit on the wrong side

Inside Marakabei's store, and an outside view, below.

of the road and sideswiped a vehicle belonging to a local African. The police, I think with a certain amount of glee, had brought a charge of reckless driving against the brother. My verdict in court was that he was guilty of dangerous driving and I would have fined him probably £10. Bob Morrison thought it was a great decision! The brother accepted it quite calmly and the Church paid up his fine.

Roman Catholic Mission Consisted of Church, School and Living Quarters

The Marakabei Roman Catholic Mission, similar to so many other Catholic Missions in the mountains, was a well constructed conglomerate of Church, school classrooms, residential buildings etc. The buildings

Roma Mission

Typical Roman Catholic Church built of sandstone with much labour supplied by "penance labour" — "Father I have sinned". Four days cutting sandstone was atonement.

were made from locally cut stone. Construction was done under the supervision of a lay brother, either Irish or, strangely enough, French Canadian. A good portion of the labour was provided in penance. The priest took Confession regularly and the penance of a certain number of days' labour in helping construct the Mission was well understood and accepted by members of the African congregation, and the Church benefitted enormously throughout Lesotho from this free labour. The Church at Marakabei had a tall sandstone tower with two huge brass bells. These bells had been transported to Marakabei before the road came through, each slung between two oxen. I understand that it was a very difficult task and there appear to have been a number of casualties amongst the beasts of burden, poor things. But the bells were mounted and called the congregants to Church every Sunday and attendance was extremely good, running into many hundreds.

The teaching facilities that the Church provided at Marakabei, as in so many other places in Lesotho, were a tremendous asset to the Church and the residences. All three of the major churches in Lesotho had teacher training schools and ninety-nine per cent of teachers at the schools were local Basotho. Not only did it provide jobs, but it also provided school facilities and one must commend the Missions for what they did, and no doubt continue to do, for the local population.

I remember meeting one of the local priests at Marakabei and he had a beautiful Alsatian dog. I commented on the dog and that he looked in such good condition. The priest seemed quite pleased about this. When I told Bob Morrison the story he said that this particular priest had a pellet gun which he used to shoot rats that ran along the rafters in the Church. He considered that a fat rat was too big a meal for his Alsatian so he used to cut the rats in half and feed the dog with half a rat at a time plus some maize meal porridge. The diet seemed to suit the dog because it certainly looked very healthy.

Medicine Murder: What is it and Why Does it Occur?

Medicine murder has always been one of the most controversial and disturbing issues in Lesotho history. These murders are not a new issue; they are known to have taken place long ago, before Europeans first arrived in Lesotho. The practice entails cutting flesh from a living victim before killing them and normally throwing the corpse over a cliff. The flesh is used to make medicines which are placed in a medicine horn, kept by the chief. Lips, eyelids and testicles were often taken.

Medicine murder was not a human sacrifice as such. The Basotho had a longstanding belief in witchcraft. There was a belief that a strong medicine horn would bring good fortune and protection from enemies. A medicine horn with human flesh in it was very powerful. In past times human flesh was obtained from victims on battlefields. With the advent of British rule the conflicts of previous years ceased and there was no longer war so it became necessary to devise new means to obtain human flesh.

Many chiefs had a medicine horn and believed it would play a big part in ensuring their success as chief and their ability to control those that they administered.

In the 1940s and 1950s there was a rash of medicine murders. This was an era in which the chiefs felt the need to find ways to withstand the ever-increasing influence of the new vocal and often educated aspiring political leaders who were seldom of chiefly background. During this time the High Court of Lesotho sentenced a number of perpetrators, including chiefs, to death for medicine murder and they all hanged. It was supposed to send out a message and be a deterrent to others. It never made the slightest difference—the sequence of murders continued, convincing me strongly that the death penalty is not a good thing. I remember a horrible occasion when fourteen Basotho men were convicted and hanged for their participation in a single medicine murder. The director of the main prison in Maseru had to attend and witness the hangings. I met him for a drink at the Maseru Club later that evening; he was a much shaken man. The mass hanging had no deterrent effect. It was not until the 1960s onwards that the frequency of medicine murders fell away sharply. In modern times it would no longer be an issue.

In my capacity as a District Commissioner and therefore also a Magistrate, I took the preliminary examinations of suspected medicine murders which culminated in the proceedings being transferred to the High Court of Lesotho for trial.

There was a huge rivalry between two factions of the royal line as to who should be appointed regent during the minority of the rightful and accepted future Paramount Chief, who was only four years old when his father died. Two senior chiefs were accused and convicted for medicine murder and both went to the gallows.

A Winter 'Trek' to Lesobeng with Captain Ken Shortt-Smith

There were occasions when my official duties required me to visit areas deep in the mountains. There were no roads so we went on horseback. On this particular occasion we had to go to Lesobeng, eight hours' ride from the road head. Captain Shortt-Smith was investigating yet another medicine murder. A mutilated body had been found at the base of a cliff and a local chief was under suspicion. The murder investigation was a police matter but I happened to have separate issues to discuss with the local Chief and it was convenient for Ken and me to travel together seeing we both had business at Lesobeng.

When on trek a District Officer would be accompanied by an interpreter, a political messenger, two pack grooms and two or three Police Troopers, each person riding their own horse, and four pack mules. When on trek I slept in a canvas tent with a stretcher, usually six blankets because it got so bitterly cold up in the mountains, my tuckbox, and food I cooked on a kerosene Primus stove. The Lesotho mountains are almost devoid of trees so one couldn't rely on the availability of wood to make a fire.

Pack mules loaded with our equipment. We used these whenever we went on "trek".

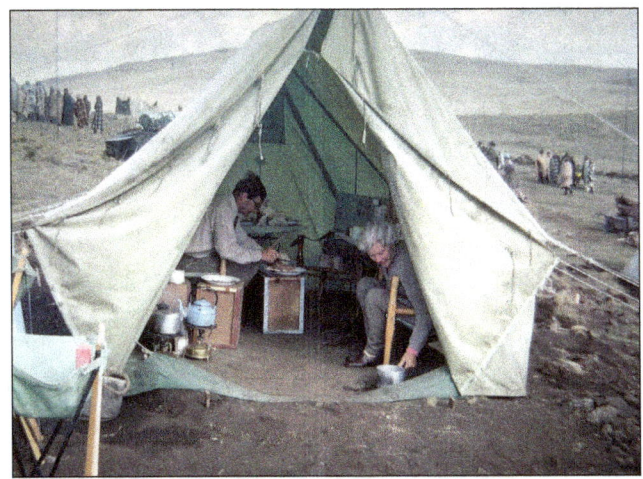

My tent on trek.

On trek — daily ablutions.

Three days ahead we sent the Police Troopers and pack grooms up to Marakabei from Maseru with all the animals and they were required to wait for us at Marakabei. We then drove to Marakabei, stayed overnight at the Resthouse and started the ride to Lesobeng the following morning.

Riding on trek requires a lot of patience. One seldom gets into more than a trot, very occasionally a canter. There's nothing more tiring than having a horse that has to be coaxed continually to keep up with the other animals. The horses and mules we used always came from the Police stables and I always tried to get a horse known as Tillard which was quite famous as a trekking horse. To get to Lesobeng we had to ride over the mountain tops separating the Mantsonyane River and the Senqunyane River and

Left to right: Chief Matlere, Mr Rasekoai, a local trader, and an agricultural officer. Chief Matlere was twice tried for medicine murder and acquitted.

then over another mountain range and down to Lesobeng. We got caught in ice-cold rain on our way to Lesobeng as we went over the highest point of the mountains. When on trips such as this or other similar rides, one is not on a road, only a mule track. On the steep slopes the track is normally built in a zig zag up the mountain using local stone and filled in with local gravel. These mule tracks were built many years back and certainly were a great asset in negotiating the mountain crossings. The horses are sure-footed and one has to place total confidence in this because in many areas one has a sheer drop on one side down into a ravine.

It was a long ride, made longer by the fact that the lead Police Trooper kept telling Ken and me that Lesobeng was just around the corner when in actual fact it turned out that it was another two hours' ride. We eventually reached our destination at dusk and put up our tents at a respectable distance and out of view of the Mission. We spent the first night in our camp and cooked a healthy meal on the Primus. It's amazing what one can do on a little Primus in a little canvas tent. It would have been meat and vegetables followed by a sweet course and we no doubt had a bit of alcoholic spirits. One would never carry beer because it's too bulky and heavy to get into saddlebags. The Primus in a fairly short time warms up the interior of the tent nicely. We ate separately from our Basotho staff.

In the morning I met up with the local headman for discussion on various topical matters; in particular there was a boundary dispute that we needed to discuss because it was causing problems. In the instance of boundary disputes, it frequently was necessary to ride the boundary with the two chiefs concerned and get agreement that in fact this was where the boundary should be. Whether you achieved agreement or not could be problematic.

In Ken's medicine murder matter, the victim was a mentally deficient person and the pattern of the murder was very much in keeping with the normal procedure. Ken came back that afternoon and said that the headman was quite belligerent towards him. Ken and I slept in separate tents and in the middle of the night Ken woke to the sound of a rustling of something trying to get into his tent. Bearing in mind his dealings with the headman that afternoon and the fact that the headman was a prime suspect in the medicine murder, Ken had gone to sleep with his police baton alongside his stretcher. As the noise persisted he quietly got his baton and took a hefty swing at the place where he perceived the noise to be coming from. It resulted in the terrified and pained howling of a dog.

Dinner at the Roman Catholic Mission

Whilst at Lesobeng we were invited to dine at the local Mission. The inhabitants were all white and consisted of a priest, a lay brother and two nuns. We were treated to a nicely prepared meal with the priest and the lay brother and were waited on by the two nuns. At no stage did the nuns sit down with us. The priest had a well-stocked kerosene fridge and he was able to offer us a good range of cordials and spirits. The Roman Catholic Church is very laid back about alcohol and I was quite surprised that we weren't offered a glass of wine as well. It was a good meal and, despite the isolation, I didn't feel too sorry for the priest and the lay brother because they were living well. The dinner conversation was very interesting because they were in close touch with the local community, spoke Sesotho fluently and knew all the local gossip.

Caught in a Snow Storm; So Very Cold on Horseback

We spent three nights at Lesobeng then headed for home. On the way back we got caught in a heavy snow storm between the Lesobeng and Senqunyane Rivers. At one stage on the higher slopes the snow was probably six to nine inches deep and our animals had to get through it all with the snow still falling. When we got over the mountain and down the other side and below the snow line, we stopped and gathered brushwood, locally known as sehalahala, and made a fire to thaw out. It was a very cold trip indeed. We got back to our vehicle pretty late, spent the night at Marakabei and drove home the next day. Our pack grooms and one Police Trooper were then required to bring the animals all the way back to Maseru, another three days' ride, and I was so glad that it was not me having to do that.

An Eventful Afternoon Stuck in the Snow on a Remote Track in the Lesotho Mountains at a Height of 11,000 feet

In August 1965 on a Sunday afternoon, Gail and I were on our way home to Mokhotlong after spending a few days in Himeville with friends. To get home, we had to get up the Sani Pass with many sharp bends and some gradients as sharp as 1:3. After successfully getting up the Sani Pass we crossed the Sani Flats at a height of 10,500 feet (about 3200 metres) and then we were set to get over the Kotisepholo Mountain Range with the road rising to 11,000ft (3300m). (Note: Mt Kosciuszko is the highest peak in Australia at a height of 7300ft (2200m).)

Once over Kotisepholo the track was all downhill to Mokhotlong and a nice warm house—but this last bit entailed another 2½ hours driving to cover 35 miles (56km).

On the last steep slope up the Kotisepholo the Land Rover was unable to get traction. The wheels simply spun and there we were on a Sunday afternoon stuck at a height of about 11,000 feet with Beverley, a four-month-old baby, on Gail's lap, well shrouded in blankets. We had about two hours of daylight left. It was not a pleasant predicament to find ourselves in and it was highly irresponsible on my part to have undertaken the trip in the circumstances as they were and which I should easily have predicted as foreseeable. What I ultimately did was to walk up the frozen strip of road with a four-gallon jerry can of petrol, pour the petrol into one track of the road and put a match to it. The petrol trickled down a good length of the track and the flame followed it down. The burning petrol did its job by melting the snow in that track and, by taking a high speed run at the track and then up, we got enough traction on the melted side of the track to get ourselves up and over.

The overnight temperature, if stuck where we were, would have gone down to minus ten degrees.

It was a big relief and a lesson to me well learned that I was now a father with a gorgeous wife and a gorgeous baby and they had to be looked after appropriately. The gung-ho bachelor days were over.

Relieving District Commissioner

In late 1957 I was sent to relieve at Mafeteng for two months as District Commissioner while the substantive incumbent, namely Rivers Thompson, was on overseas leave. I moved into his house which was a big sandstone place with an even bigger garden. I had four prisoners working in the garden and I took over the Thompson servants.

I never liked Mafeteng much. It is a dusty little village and I always found the local chiefs a bit bolshy. It didn't help when you were only 25 years old and taking charge of a district of probably 150,000 people at that time, with responsibility for the court work. By that stage I had passed all my exams and my jurisdiction had been increased to two years' imprisonment with an option to impose four years in stock theft cases.

The local police officer was Captain Monty Williams, a very British, moustachioed gentleman. Not long after my stay in Mafeteng (I can assure you I had nothing to do with it) he and his wife suddenly produced a son after twenty years of childless marriage.

We had a mutual interest in duckshooting which helped and we would at weekends, on occasion, go out to a couple of local dams where there was good duck and goose shooting. It was summer and I played cricket for the local Mafeteng side. However there was not much social life and I would often go down to Maseru for a weekend. The road was not sealed and the fifty-odd miles seemed a very long way in those days.

I look back in amazement at my audacity during those months as Acting District Commissioner, aged 25, in conducting a very resolute anti-soil-erosion exercise in the mountain foothills. In Lesotho soil erosion is a big problem because the rain comes in the form of heavy summer falls and the water rushes down the mountainsides and carries the soil away. The situation is much aggravated by the fact that with the ever-growing population there is ever-increasing pressure on the land; more and more people want to own the same number of animals as the people next door so the number of animals grows, the countryside gets overgrazed, and the grass and undergrowth protection of the mountain slopes deteriorates. As a result, the agricultural authorities in Lesotho, under Les Collett and later taken over by Sid Youthed, constructed a system of contour banks on the mountain slopes which proved very effective if properly maintained. Legislation was introduced to make it an offence not to maintain your contour banks and in some cases prohibiting grazing in certain areas at certain times.

In this particular area in the Mafeteng District there was blatant disregard of soil erosion regulations and I conducted a court in a village in the foothills where I convicted a lot of the leading African citizens of the area who, in some cases, declined to pay their fines, so I sent them to jail. I can remember meeting up with the local European trading store manager and he was laughing and saying, "Well you know, so and so and so and so are just not going to be very happy." I think it was an exercise which in later years I would have been very hesitant to conduct but I guess the bravado of youth prevailed and I was fortunate in that I was only going to be in the District for three months or so.

I also had a run-in with Rivers Thompson's maid who had been with them for twenty-five years and who considered that she was the real boss in the house in the absence of her employers. She used to come to me with the orders for provisions such as sugar and mealie meal (maize meal) for the servants and all the everyday requirements to run the household and feed both myself and the servants. I was pretty ignorant in those days about the requirements and after about a month when we seemed to be getting through pounds and pounds of sugar every week, I realised that something was not right. I remonstrated with the maid but in the next couple of weeks things didn't improve, so I sacked her. I had learned that the sugar was being used in alcoholic brews in her beer hall in the village at my expense. The fact that I sacked her really set her back on her heels and later in the day she came back and pleaded with me for reinstatement. I said, "No, I'm sorry, you'll have to wait until the Rivers Thompsons come back." When her employers did eventually return they were very taken aback that their maid of twenty-five years had been sacked by me and I'm not sure that they really accepted the whole situation as I explained it to them. However in the long run it didn't seem to affect our relationship. Some years later after Gail and I were married I can recall going to dinner with the Rivers Thompsons in Maseru and this particular maid had cooked the meal and was serving at the dinner table. She gave me a look and I returned the look and wondered whether arsenic was going to be put in my coffee.

After those three months in Mafeteng, where I must have performed reasonably well, I became the Relieving District Commissioner for the next eighteen months. My next position was at Quthing. This location is in the far south of Lesotho and is a most interesting district.

Once again the District Commissioner's house was large and built of sandstone. By this time I had acquired a good set of cutlery, crockery, cooking utensils, linen etc. I was glad that I had learned to deal with social entertainment, largely due to my experience when I was being brought up in Botswana and Mafeking. It was extremely useful knowing how to prepare nice snacks for cocktail parties and I'd learnt to do a bit of cooking, although I had a cook who was pretty good and fed me well. During that stage I found myself having to entertain and put up for a night Archbishop Joost de Blanc, the Archbishop of Cape Town, who was a well-known figure because of his outspoken attitude towards apartheid in South Africa. There were also visits by judges, senior Government officials, and on occasions personal friends. I received some very nice letters from people such as the Archbishop and Government Secretary thanking and commending me on the way they had been looked after.

It was on this particular tour of duty at Quthing that I had to deal with a very nasty student strike at Leloaleng Trade School. This trade school was well known for the calibre of young African tradesmen it was training. There were approximately sixty students, all of them boarders and coming from all parts of Lesotho. The dispute appeared to have arisen from complaints about food and had then escalated into a confrontation between staff and a certain segment of the students. I worked closely with the local African Police Officer and my Political Messenger, Sergeant George.

I went down to the school accompanied by the Police Officer and the Political Messenger (liaison officer) and talked to the students in the hall about their grievances. There was a certain group who were obviously very intimidatory to the rest of the students and there was no compromise, and as I walked out of the hall I was pulled back by the Police Officer because the ringleader was standing in my way with a metal bar in his hand. The Police Officer and the Political Messenger remonstrated with him and he let me through and so we went back to the offices. There was an obvious threat of violence. I had kept on good terms with the local chiefs so I commandeered five public works department lorries and sent members of my staff out on each lorry into the villages to make contact with the headmen and where necessary the local chiefs and discuss what was happening, and request that he encourage every able-bodied man in the village to get into the vehicles and come into Quthing so that we could put toether a formidable group of men sufficiently intimidatory to persuade the students to give up their strike. A few hours later every vehicle returned with a full load of men carrying sticks, knobkerries and various other rather intimidatory weapons. The men were placed under the control of the Police Officer and the Political Messenger and the senior local chief was there as well. We once again got into discussions with the group and advised them that we were requiring them to return home. In the meantime I had hired a bus which carried sixty-six passengers and we herded all the students into the bus. The majority of them were going northwards and so I guess about fifty went in the bus and the local students quietly dispersed.

With that large group of rather threatening vigilantes in the background there was no further threatening behaviour from the striking group. Word had got through to headquarters in Maseru about what was happening and the Commissioner of Police in Maseru had contacted the

South African Police with a request that their border police should get the bus through the border quickly and allow it to travel through South Africa and then back into Lesotho further up the line. This happened and the South African Police were very helpful. I received many complimentary letters from my seniors in Maseru which was very gratifying. This particular exercise stood me in good stead in enabling me to deal with a very big generational strike that took place in Maseru three years later when I was District Commissioner in charge there.

From Quthing I was sent to relieve at Mokhotlong, a mountain district with no roads, only jeep tracks. It was quite an experience. It was 1958 and the tracks coming up the Sani Pass were still in a developmental stage. The Sani Pass in those days was still little more than a jeep track. The track comes up from Underberg in Natal from the base of the Drakensberg escarpment up to the top of the Pass. The track rises 3000 feet in two miles (almost 1000m in three kilometres). To get up one could only use a 4WD vehicle. In a long wheel base Land Rover twenty-six reverses were required to get up to the top of the Pass because the corners were so tight. Vehicles were fitted with a hand throttle thus leaving your feet totally free to use the brakes. Often the Pass was covered in snow and the corners facing south during winter could be very icy and slippery. It was normal to go down the Pass every few weeks to collect provisions not only for oneself but for one's servants. The journey from Mokhotlong camp to the Sani Pass Hotel at the bottom of the Pass took three and a half hours to cover forty-four miles (70km). At the highest point the track rose to just over 11,000ft (3300m) and my house was approximately 8000ft (2500m) above sea level.

I enjoyed the journeys down to the base of the Pass because I had friends who ran the rather precarious transport service at the Pass and they lived down in Natal and we always had a good party at the Sani Hotel or at their houses or at the Sani Pass Hotel. There was also good partridge shooting in winter. A group of probably three of us would go out on horseback and ride out the partridge on the mountain slopes. You would then dismount and walk the partridge out. They sat very tight and would get up in a flurry of wings right under your feet and they were not always easy to shoot. One would never shoot a partridge on the ground, it always had to be flying. They were very good eating and on many a weekend I had good partridge shooting.

My house at Mokhotlong consisted of a three-bedroom dwelling made of local stone. It was a very adequate house but in winter it was an extremely cold place. The lowest temperature recorded during my two stints at Mokhotlong was minus 40º Fahrenheit.

I was in Mokhotlong from approximately July to September 1959 and it was winter and very cold. Living at the height we did, we had some very cold spells. I always wore wool-lined shoes because the ground was often quite cold and my feet were what suffered most. The house was reasonably warm so long as all the possible cracks through which the cold air could get in were blocked. For instance, the windows were totally sealed during winter and we had door stops and every single device to ensure that no wind got in from outside. The stove burned anthracite and heated the hot water for the bathroom as well and worked efficiently. In my sitting room I had an anthracite slow combustion burner and I kept this going constantly. The anthracite came up the Sani Pass in a Land Rover and I was responsible for my own costs in that respect. A bag of anthracite cost £3 in those days and that was a lot of money, so whenever I went down the Pass in my own vehicle I would always bring back a couple of bags. Kerosene was also important because all the lamps were the pressure type and these worked on kerosene.

I had two servants and providing them with food was my responsibility so I would also ensure that when going down the Sani Pass I brought back a bag of maize meal weighing 200 pounds (90kg).

The Mokhotlong village consisted of mainly Government houses. These houses accommodated those of us who were employed by the Basutoland Government. The employees worked either at the Hospital, Agriculture Department, Post Office, Police, District Office Administration etc, and there would have been about thirty of these houses. There were four big houses, one each for the District Commissioner, the Police Officer, the Doctor and the Agricultural Officer.

There was no electricity in any of the houses, not even the Disrict Commissioner's house at that time. All lighting at night was by way of kerosene lamps or candles. Water was reticulated into the houses. There was a natural spring about three miles away up a little valley and the water was brought down to the village in an open furrow then into a big concrete storage tank, from where it went into a pipe system which reticulated into the houses. The watering system was quite good because the excess water—once the storage tank was full—was furrowed down to the houses of the Police Officer and District Commissioner and it was therefore possible to have a nice garden, particularly in view of the privilege of having four prisoners working in the garden. The asparagus bed at the District Commissioner's house in Mokhotlong was superb in the spring.

In addition to the residential houses there was the District Commissioner's Office, the Hospital with two wards, one male and one female, each accommodating ten patients. My office consisted of a big office for myself, four offices for clerical staff and a reasonably sized Courtroom which was also used for community purposes such as concerts. The jail in those days was quite medieval and could house about forty prisoners. It was built of stone with very dark cells and it must have been very cold in winter. There was one trading store owned by Ridgeway and de la Harpe.

Private Secretary to Sir John Maud
British High Commissioner to South Africa

In the second half of 1959 I was advised that I had been appointed to the position of Private Secretary to the British High Commissioner. The High Commission office was situated in Cape Town for the first half of the year and in Pretoria for the second half. I was at that time a District Officer in Maseru. I was both surprised and flattered.

Sir John and Lady (Jean) Maud, 1960

On my return from six weeks' overseas leave, I reported to the British High Commission early in January. At that stage Sir John and Lady Maud had not arrived so it gave me a couple of weeks to settle in. My predecessor as Private Secretary was Peter Bridges. He had been Private Secretary to Sir Percivale Liesching. It was fortuitous that we overlapped for a couple of weeks as he was able to show me the ropes. It was obviously going to be a very different existence to that of a District Officer in Lesotho.

I found myself a flat in Rosebank, a Cape Town suburb well placed to drive to both the High Commission Office and to the High Commissioner's residence in Wynberg.

The new High Commissioner duly arrived by sea in mid-January and I well recall going down to meet him. He was with Lady Maud and their youngest daughter, aged about eighteen, called Ginny. Sir John came with a formidable reputation as an administrator and orator and a man of great intellectual capacity. During the war he had made a name for himself as Secretary to the Ministry of Munitions. He had subsequently occupied a number of positions in the British Govern-ment and had also held various academic positions. He was rated as one of the best five after-dinner speakers in the United Kingdom.

He was a man of great charm but I can't say that I ever really felt totally at ease and in harmony with him. Lady Maud had been a concert pianist in her earlier days and still regarded herself as a professional pianist. She had a mass of red hair and was quite eccentric. They were both kind people but I can't say it was a particularly easy relationship, and my eighteen months as Private Secretary I do not regard as being one of my best work performances, although I certainly didn't disgrace myself.

High Commission House in Cape Town was a big double-storey building in Wynberg with many bedrooms and many bathrooms and lots of entertainment areas. The gardens were beautiful and huge and there was the inevitable black Rolls Royce with a chauffeur, Vincent, in a traditional dark blue chauffeur's uniform with peaked cap. The Mauds had recruited a white butler in England called James and he was an awful man. He was ex-Army and exploited his position as butler. He caused us lots of problems by using a car with diplomatic number plates which he parked in no-parking areas. The authorities would contact me and complain but of course would not issue a ticket because of the diplomatic number plates. No matter how often I remonstrated with him, a few weeks later he would do the same thing. Eventually he learnt how to intimidate Lady Maud and he was downright rude to her. Why on earth they would not agree to sack him, I don't know. The rest of the staff were African and were very good, certainly streets ahead of the white butler.

In those days there was an unusual arrangement in South Africa which necessitated that diplomatic missions spend six months in Cape Town and six months in Pretoria. The reason was that the parliamentary sessions in South Africa were held in the Houses of Parliament in Cape Town and then for the second half of the year when parliament did not meet, everyone would move up to Pretoria which was the executive capital of South Africa. The reason for this split situation was that at the time of Union of the four different colonies and republics which made up South Africa (Cape Colony, Natal, Orange Free State, Transvaal), there was argument as to where the capital should be located. The people of the inland area, namely Transvaal and the Orange Free State, wanted the capital to be in Pretoria and the two coastal states wanted it to be in Cape Town. The compromise was that the Houses of Parliament would be established in Cape Town (the legislative capital) and would sit from February to July, and then the conduct of Government would be moved to Pretoria (the executive capital). The Union buildings in Pretoria were built at the time of Union, designed by Sir Herbert Baker, and are a truly magnificent architectural design. So, to achieve harmony between all parties in 1910 when the Union of South Africa came into being, the country was landed with this cumbersome process of moving the trappings of government and the diplomatic corps back and forth every six months.

The distance between Cape Town and Pretoria is approximately 1600 kilometres. Each Minister and all the ministerial staff who had to be available required offices and housing in both Cape Town and Pretoria. The same went for the diplomatic corps. The British High Commission,

Union Buildings, Pretoria—seat of Executive Parliamentary Authority in South Africa. This building designed by Sir Herbert Baker is by any standards a beautiful building.

Senate Building, Cape Town, as it was in 1960. Under the new South African constitution the Senate no longer exists.

in accordance with this arrangement, had an office in both places and also residences. For half the year the offices were simply retained on a caretaker basis, likewise the main residences. For persons like myself, a bachelor in my late twenties, it was great to be able to spend six months down near the sea in a beautiful city like Cape Town and then when the cold, wet winter set in, to move northwards to the warm winter sun of Pretoria.

One of my first tasks as Private Secretary was to make the necessary arrangements for Sir John to meet senior South African Government officials and also to make courtesy calls on all the High Commissioners and Ambassadors of other diplomatic missions. In those days there were thirty-five diplomatic missions at ambassadorial or high commission level in South Africa. Those first few weeks for Sir John, and I guess for myself, were very much devoted to getting to know people and getting to know what the job was about.

I had some involvement with Lady Maud's diary. Her solo piano recitals could be embarrassing. She had once been a recognised pianist but that was years back. She never came to terms with this. On one occasion she was asked by Mrs Jansen, the Governor-General's wife, to play at a charity concert. When she learnt she would be sharing the stage with others she declined. Sir John was very embarrassed and asked me to contact the Governor-General's office and advise them that Lady Maud would be delighted to accept Mrs Jansen's invitation. It was too late, Mrs Jansen had withdrawn the invitation and never asked Lady Maud again.

Sir John's duties were divided into two distinct components. Firstly, he was the British High Commissioner to South Africa and in this respect performed his diplomatic duties. Secondly he was High Commissioner for the three high commission territories, namely Basutoland, Bechuanaland Protectorate and Swaziland. In the latter regard he was equivalent to the Governor. The three territories were British-controlled and came under the authority of the British Colonial Office. Policy guidelines determined which responsibilities Sir John could administer himself and what had to be referred back to the British authorities in London. In each of the three territories there was a Resident Commissioner who was the senior local official and had considerable authority to administer the affairs of the territory for which he had charge. The responsibilities of Sir John necessitated that he visit each territory periodically. About four weeks after his arrival

Sir John on official visit to Maseru, Lesotho, in 1962.
L-R: King Moshoeshoe, Sir John Maud and Sir Alexander Giles (Resident Commissioner, Lesotho)

in Cape Town a trip was arranged to visit Basutoland, Swaziland and then on to Durban. I was very much involved in making the arrangements but unfortunately about a week before we were due to leave I was laid low by a severe inner ear problem which later developed into Meniere's disease. I got out of bed one morning and fell down, quite unable to stand, and this lasted for a few weeks. It was three weeks before I could join Sir John in Durban. It was disappointing because I would have enjoyed being with him on his first visit to Basutoland which I knew so well.

When the High Commissioner visited the high commission territories he travelled in a Royal Air Force Dove aircraft. The British High Commission had a military attaché section which was staffed by a Royal Air Force Group Captain and a Flight Lieutenant who flew the aircraft. The Group Captain had special diplomatic responsibilities in establishing liaisons with military counterparts in South Africa and this was regarded as part of the whole British apparatus for maximum liaison with South Africa. I have no doubt the military aspect also had certain commercial

De Havilland Dove. The United Kingdom retained a military attaché in South Africa which had an intelligence and military equipment sales function. The Dove aircraft was based permanently in Pretoria and was available for the use of the British High Commissioner on special occasions.

facets. The Dove aircraft was a two-engined passenger plane which could carry about twelve people.

When I joined Sir John on the Durban/Pietermaritzburg section of his trip, the Rolls Royce had been sent from Cape Town for his three days in Durban. Having the black Rolls Royce was all part of the image of the top British official in South Africa. The Rolls did provide that extra image. The only drawback was when something went wrong, as happened in the following year after I had left the British High Commissioner and returned to Basutoland: the Rolls Royce broke down in the main street of Port Elizabeth with the High Commissioner in it. What an image for a black Rolls Royce!

Sir John's reputation as an orator had spread before his arrival in South Africa and he was much in demand for dinners such as Chambers of Commerce, agricultural shows, mayors' banquets, etc. In Durban we stayed at the Caister Hotel near the seafront. It was one of those old, staid hotels that seemed to appeal to the Mauds. I didn't think it was very good but they felt comfortable there. Sir John attended a number of dinners and also was guest speaker at the Natal Royal Agricultural Show held in Pietermaritzburg. When making a speech he was quite amazing: he had a photographic memory and studied his speech before the occasion and then could quote reams and reams of figures and statistics with never a

Rolls Royce Silver Cloud. Every British High Commissioner or Ambassador is chauffeured around in a black Rolls Royce. On one occasion our beautiful Rolls splintered its differential in the main street of Port Elizabeth on a much-publicised official visit to that city—black oil all over the street and an embarrassed Sir John stranded—great publicity for an iconic British product.

note in front of him, and he never slipped up. One of the principles to which he adhered in public speaking was that to make people listen you had to make them laugh and he was good at that. He would put in a good joke and get people laughing and then follow it up with a really important fact or statement of British policy.

Sir John was a very religious man and went to church three or four times a week. His sister was the Mother Superior of an English convent in Pretoria. He was the son of a Bishop and his brother was a Bishop. I remember one of his jokes which he told at the Pietermaritzburg Agricultural Show. I can't remember how it came in but he talked about some lady who had laying hens and the price she was being offered was not very good and she finally said, "My hens are not going to wreck their arses for ninepence a dozen." It gained a big laugh. I can't quite remember how the joke and the speech fitted together but it was typical of him that sometimes he would go quite close to etiquette boundaries in the jokes that he told.

On these trips it was my responsibility to ensure that Sir John was properly briefed on the background to every function he attended, whom he was likely to meet and who those people were, with background notes, times of arrival and departure, and on occasion I would even try to obtain an advance copy of the table plan so that Sir John knew who he was going to be sitting next to so that he could be properly briefed on every single person within talking distance of him. A lot of these notes I would not be able to write myself but would have to contact the right people and ensure that all the background information was co-ordinated into an easily read document. On occasions he would attend half a dozen functions in a day and this entailed a great deal of work for me. I would do as much as I could before departure from the High Commission Office in Cape Town or Pretoria and then I would have to garner information as I went along. There was a lot of detective work involved.

Sir John wrote many of his own speeches but he still needed a lot of facts and figures before he put his speech together. I remember one particular occasion about three months after I had joined the High Commission Office when I discovered that I had booked him for a Chamber of Commerce dinner in Port Elizabeth and at the same time it was imperative that he be at a meeting with South African authorities in Cape Town. I went into his office and told him that I appeared to have made a really bad mistake. He got up from his seat, came round to my side of the desk, put his arm round my shoulder and said, "Come on Ted, now let's just see how we can work this out." The way we worked it out was to contact the Port Elizabeth Chamber of Commerce and request that, because for unavoidable diplomatic reasons Sir John would not be able to attend their function on that particular day, could it be switched to another day. There was time enough to get the date switched and they were very nice about it, to my great relief.

In the High Commission office the staff consisted of the High Commissioner (Sir John) and two Deputy High Commissioners, one on the diplomatic side and the other on the high commission territory side (Basutoland, Bechuanaland Protectorate and Swaziland). On each side of the office there were a series of first secretaries, second secretaries, third secretaries and then all the more junior staff associated with the everyday running of the office. In total there would have been about twenty young ladies associated with Registry, typing, telephones, etc. The Administrative Officer who was responsible for recruitment must have paid considerable attention to looks because these young ladies really were a bevy of beauties. However, in that first five months in the office I tended to take out girls not associated with the office and it was not until I reached Pretoria in the second part of the year that I took much notice of the girls within the office. Liz Tennant from Basutoland days had come down to Cape Town and was a first-year nurse and I did start to see a bit of her, but she then gave up nursing and went to stay with her parents at George which is about four hundred kilometres from Cape Town. My MG Magnet was a good car for long trips and I used to cruise up the coast to George every now and then. Liz's parents had a small farm near George, a lovely spot, and I enjoyed the break when I visited her.

Liz Tennant—later married Ken Shortt-Smith.

Our association became quite serious and when the office moved to Pretoria in July, Liz also moved back to Basutoland. I used to go down to Basutoland on occasions to visit her and she used to come up to Pretoria. Liz was and still is a delightful person with a great sense of humour and extremely capable. She is an outstanding horsewoman. When our affair reached a certain stage I think we probably both realised that it wasn't the best. She married Ken Shortt-Smith. She was the ideal person for Ken because he was a really nice man and had been widowed, leaving three children ranging in ages from about seven to fourteen, and Liz was the sort of person who was admirably suited to taking over the household. She did this in her usual calm and capable way and played a tremendous part in the success of the three children, and she and Ken also had two children of their own. Ken died of cancer in 1990 or thereabouts and Liz lives on the family property which she inherited at George in South Africa.

As Private Secretary I had an office adjacent to that of the High Commissioner and in this fairly spacious office I had two ladies working with me. Clodah Coy and Noel Anderson were old hands who had been with the office for a long time and it was great to have them alongside to guide me when necessary. Both were spinsters and Clodah in particular was a very forthright person but very nice.

During this period the High Commissioner undertook a trip to Bechuanaland. He flew in the RAF Dove aircraft. We visited Maun, Kanye and Serowe. Flying over the great Makarikari Salt Pans was a memorable experience because there had been exceptional rains and all the game had moved down south from the Okavango area. Visiting Botswana was a special occasion for me because I knew the country well but had grown to know it in a very different capacity. When we flew from the Makarikari down to Serowe, where the plane was scheduled to land at 1.00pm, the pilot got thoroughly lost. I remember sitting in the plane and the pilot admitting he was lost and that he would have to cut across due east to intersect with the railway line, get his bearings and then find his way to Serowe. Sitting in that plane I recognised the Swaneng Hills which are close to Serowe. We always called them Mother Swaneng, Baby Swaneng and Daddy Swaneng because there were the three hills of different size alongside one another. Things look different from the air and I told the pilot that I was pretty sure they were the Swaneng Hills but in the circumstances it probably was safer to go across to the railway line and get his bearings; I knew that it was only forty-odd miles across to the railway line if the hills were in fact what I said they were.

At this stage a junior officer who was travelling in the plane as part of our group was air sick all over the back of the Group Captain who was not at all pleased. He was going to have to meet a lot of important people on the airstrip at Serowe in a short time and he was going to smell and his uniform was going to look pretty awful. We duly got to Serowe two hours late just as they were about to send out a search party. There was no radio communication between the aircraft and Serowe because everyone was out at the airstrip and in those days it was simply an airstrip with a little tin hut and nothing else.

We stayed overnight at Serowe and a cocktail party was given by the District Commissioner of that time who was living in the house on the hill which I knew so well and which we used to live in. Sir Seretse and Lady Ruth Khama were there. By this time the politics of Bechuanaland had changed completely and Seretse and Ruth had returned and he was once again a very eminent person in Bechuanaland, rightfully so. However, the wounds obviously had not fully healed because at the cocktail party when I was introduced to Ruth Khama in the official line-up, she said, "Are you the son of *the* Nettelton?" I replied that I was and she turned on her heel and walked away without shaking hands. (Note: Dad had been a member of the three-man Judicial Commission which was instrumental in having Seretse Khama banished from Botswana in 1950.) In later years when Sir Seretse Khama became Chancellor of the University of Basutoland, Lesotho, Botswana and Swaziland I had dealings (in my capacity as Secretary to Chief Leabua, the Prime Minister) with them when I was back in Lesotho and we re-established good relations; in fact I think we got to like one another quite a lot and she was most courteous to me.

When the High Commission office moved to Pretoria in July of that year I found accommodation at the Swartkopjes Country Club. I had a big room and ate in the club dining room. It was a pleasant location about twenty miles outside Pretoria. After about six weeks I moved to a flat in Pretoria which was more convenient and which enabled me to do my own entertaining.

The British High Commission in Pretoria was in Hill Street, in an old residence which had been converted. It was a nice location with big grounds and a tennis court. I had a nice office at the base of the main stairs and with all of those beautiful girls going up and down the stairs, I had at times to force myself to concentrate on what was on my desk instead of gazing at those beautiful legs as they went up and down the staircase. I travelled a lot with Sir John and sometimes Lady Maud came along as well. I didn't always enjoy the trips because I always felt that the Private Secretary job was not really the sort of work I wanted to do for the rest of my life, but I realised how lucky I was and what a wonderful experience it was. An interesting aspect of being Private Secretary is that every person treats you with tremendous cordiality because they know that you have the ear of the High Commissioner at all times. There were times when people were quite devious in wanting to get a view or a message through to Sir John. As Private Secretary one had tremendous power in the ability

British High Commission Office, Pretoria where I worked in 1959-1960 when Private Secretary to Sir John Maud, British High Commissioner to South Africa (pictured during a later visit with one of my daughters).

to quarantine the High Commissioner from outsiders and it would often be your own decision as to whether someone could be fitted in to see him or not, so I guess people realised this and made sure that they were always on good terms with me.

In the Private Office I had access to hugely secret files. I saw the private and confidential assessments of every single member of the office, from Deputy High Commissioner downwards, Resident Commissioners who had previously been my very senior bosses—one saw it all. I saw so many ultra-secret documents and I had to know how to keep my mouth shut. 1959 was a very delicate time in the relationship between South Africa and the UK. Apartheid was reaching new heights and this was causing strains. It was also realised that South Africa was thinking of leaving the British Commonwealth (before they got kicked out) but Britain desperately wanted to keep them within the fold because it felt that in such circumstances there would be a better chance of influencing South Africa in its policies. In fact Sir John was selected as High Commissioner because of his diplomatic skills. In a very minor sort of way I believe that a factor in my choice as Private Secretary was that I had been to school and university in South Africa, I knew South Africa well and I spoke reasonable Afrikaans. Dr Verwoerd was at that time Prime Minister of South Africa and he was pushing very hard for the ultimate achievement of apartheid in that non-Europeans would enjoy no political rights in South Africa, but they would have rights in their own homelands which comprised a very small area of South Africa and for the most part in very under-developed areas.

In the time that I spent in Pretoria I had an excellent social life. For the first six weeks or so I was still visiting Liz Tennant and she would come up and see me in Pretoria but when that broke up I found myself taking an interest in the girls in the office. Gail joined the High Commission Office about August that year. At first she was just another beautiful girl amongst a whole bevy of beauties, but I do remember remarking to one of the lesser staff members that I reckoned she had the best swing of the kilt in the whole office. One couldn't help noticing her legs when she went up the stairs. I attended a lot of social functions not of an official nature whilst in Pretoria and I became friendly with a certain Ann Clogg.

Dr Hendrik Verwoerd shaped the apartheid regime's ideology and racial policies. He was a brilliant man with all the wrong philosophies. He was murdered on the floor of the South African parliament in 1966 by a white man never previously heard of.

She was barely twenty and I was at that stage twenty-nine but we got on well together and I often went out to visit her at her parents' home. We seemed to be getting on pretty well but then I discovered that she had another boyfriend tucked away in the background; he was studying overseas at the time, and he returned and I rather think that I got dropped. She later married him. He was a biochemist and had been completing his Masters.

After the most enjoyable episode with Ann, Gail came into the picture. I can remember consulting with my two advisers in the Private Office, Clodah and Noel, asking for their advice because I had to go to a dinner party and Ann was no longer available; I sought their advice as to who they would recommend. They both recommended Gail so I got on to the telephone within the office and asked her if she would come to dinner with me on the Saturday night, to which she replied that she thought I must have got the wrong line and was it really her that I wanted to speak to. I assured her it was Gail Turner that I was wanting to invite out and she then said that her mother kept her social diary for her and she would have to check to see whether she was already booked or not. I suggested that she phone me back as soon as possible and she said she would. She in fact phoned me back very quickly and said that she would love to come out with me on that Saturday evening. The dinner was with Roy Davey and his wife who were old university friends of mine. It was just the four of us and we had a really excellent evening. I well remember the dress that Gail wore because she had a beautiful figure and she looked pretty good. On the way home she got quite cross with me because I had probably had too much to drink and was driving my MG Magnet with my hands reversed on the steering wheel, no doubt showing off, and she reckoned that it was dangerous and so I guess I tried to be the big larrikin. Anyway, it was a good start but we had quite a bumpy relationship over the next year until the time of our marriage.

I will always remember fondly those times in Pretoria even though I didn't really enjoy the job that much. I made many friends and had an excellent social time and of course the stature which one had as Private Secretary was a big image boost. Another bonus was access to duty-free goods. I could buy a case of the best French brandy and it cost me £1 per bottle. The best gin and whiskey could be obtained at a couple of pounds per bottle. Yes, the availability of the very best liquor at peppercorn prices was quite a bonus.

Eventually Stephen Henn replaced me as Private Secretary and he was much better suited to the job. He enjoyed that sort of life and did a good job. Sir John was very nice to me in that when I felt that I had stayed a decent period of time with him and approached him about going back to the Colonial Service, he asked me to think about which country I would prefer to go to and he would try to ensure that I went where I wanted to go. I was quite happy to go back to Lesotho.

In the early part of 1960 I returned to Lesotho and I was happy to be back in an environment where I felt at home. My experience in the Diplomatic Service had been exciting and in many respects very rewarding. I was fortunate to have had that rare opportunity, something which not many of my fellow District Officer colleagues ever had the opportunity to enjoy. It was a life of sophistication and glamour and the position of

Gail and me with her Austin Healey Sprite in front of her family home in Pretoria.

Private Secretary brought much prestige with it, but I nonetheless never felt entirely at home in that environment. There were so many things that I learnt and found immensely useful to me in the future. The insight into how the diplomatic world functioned, and in particular how the High Commission Office which had ultimate responsibility for Basutoland worked, and the many personalities who exercised power in those offices were all strung together gave me a rare overview of how Lesotho and the British Colonial Service were linked and how the whole thing operated.

During that time as Private Secretary I met many people of considerable prominence. I'd seen them deliberating, or round a conference table, and they were no longer just names but faces and persons and I had actually met and observed conducting their affairs in as much as they affected the British Government. Many of them I liked, others I came away feeling contempt for. One of the interesting aspects was that almost invariably those prominent figures who were really men of stature always had time to greet a Private Secretary as if he were just another human being with a status in life, whereas those figures who really were upstarts totally ignored the very existence of the more junior officials and concentrated entirely on trying to impress the "boss".

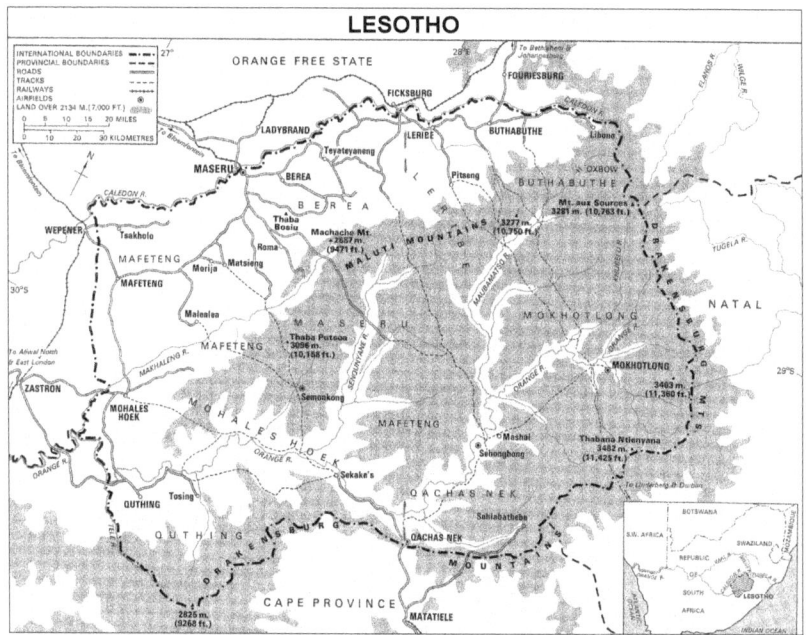

What Did a District Commissioner Do?

In my memoir I frequently bring in my role as a District Commissioner in Lesotho, and readers could be forgiven for wondering what this position involved. So I have set out here the sort of responsibilities a District Commissioner had to shoulder. It was an exciting job, the work never the same two days running. A DC, to succeed, had to be good at what he did both at his desk and in the field—and he needed to be a good communicator. To be a good DC was not for the fainthearted. I enjoyed every minute of my time as a District Commissioner and I can sit back with satisfaction because I was proud of my achievements. I was given charge of Maseru, the biggest and most volatile district, at the age of twenty-nine. I moved on to a higher appointment at the age of thirty-four.

Government Structure

In Lesotho there were nine districts, each with a District Commissioner in charge who was therefore the senior representative of the British Government in his district.

British Colonial policy was first articulated by Lord Lugard in the latter part of the nineteenth century at the time when European countries were scrambling to annex new colonies. The policy basically was to build on and work with existing indigenous structures, not break them down. The role of the District Commissioner was therefore to work with local chiefs and headmen, but there was never any ambiguity as to the fact that it was the DC who was ultimately in charge. In each district there was a range of government officers, ie agriculture, medical, education, post office, road works, prisons, police, etc. Each section ran their own "show" and maintained direct links with their departmental seniors in the capital, Maseru. A good District Commissioner would keep in close touch with every departmental representative and know what they were doing and if they were having any problems or were planning any initiatives. Where appropriate he would, as the senior government officer, have the right to become involved in the affairs of any departmental officer where broader administrative concepts were at issue.

A DC also had certain defined responsibilities, as follows:

Magistrate for the District

Advanced governmental law exams had to be passed. We dealt mainly with criminal matters but also with certain civil matters. Jurisdiction was to a maximum of two years' imprisonment and an appropriate fine, with four years in stock theft cases. In more serious cases, such as rape or murder, we would conduct a preliminary examination in court and the depositions taken were sent for examination by a judge in Maseru. If a trial resulted, all proceedings would be transferred to Maseru for hearing in a senior court. In Mokhotlong I spent on average two to three full days a week in court.

Tribal Court

Running parallel to the District Commissioner's court was a system of tribal courts. In Mokhotlong District there would have been four such courts located in different places. These courts had jurisdiction in civil matters up to a certain level. They had no criminal jurisdiction. Litigants in tribal courts had a right of appeal, not to the District Commissioner, but to a Judicial Commissioner appointed by Government.

Remands

All detainees had to be brought before the District Commissioner for remand. Remands were important in the sense that a prisoner awaiting trial could spend quite a long time in gaol waiting for his/her case to come to court. The nature of the terrain, which was mountainous with few roads, and most investigators' work having to be done on horseback by the police, meant that processes moved slowly. A detainee awaiting trial could not be held for more than fourteen days without being brought back before the District Commissioner as presiding Magistrate for review. Remands could stretch out to ten weeks at times.

In a serious case of stock theft I would have to balance a whole lot of issues when deciding whether to allow a further remand or not. I had to take into account the genuine problems of investigative work experienced by the police. I knew that a stock thief released on bail would be able to disappear into the mountains and was unlikely to front up on a summons. Then there was the principle of respect for the civil rights of the detainee. All angles had to be balanced. I believe we worked out a fair balance.

Gaol

Each district gaol had a gaoler, prison warders, cooks, cleaners, etc. In Mokhotlong we averaged a prison population of sixty. I inspected the gaol, accompanied by the gaoler, once a week, and dealt with prisoner complaints and any serious disciplinary matters brought to me involving prison warders or prisoners.

Citizen Complaints

My office door was always open to anyone who wanted to lodge a complaint.

Marriage Officer

Most weddings were conducted by church priests but I had a fair sprinkling of couples who preferred a civil marriage, and a District Commissioner was a legally gazetted Marriage Officer.

An elaborate Lesotho wedding. This Afrikaans couple were married by Dad at Maun in the early 1920s. They lived at Thanzi, way out in the western desert. They wanted a legally recognised marriage and Maun was the closest place to find a marriage officer — Dad. They trekked 300 miles by one wagon through sand country which took two to three months and then the same home!

Civil Strife

The District Commissioner was responsible for co-ordinating a response to any serious riots or strikes. In Mokhotlong I had no serious strife to deal with but when I was District Commissioner in Maseru I had to deal with a serious strike with armed gangs roaming the streets, which lasted for three days but which we resolved peacefully. On another occasion we had serious riots resulting in a police response with tear gas and baton charges.

As District Commissioner I had prime responsibility to decide on courses of action to be followed, working closely with the police and, in some cases, in consultation with African political leaders.

Then there were boundary disputes where I had, on occasion, to ride the boundary with the disputing parties to try to get agreement and calm the situation. In one dispute I rode into a situation (with a police escort) where huts were burning and three dead bodies lay around, the guts of one being eaten by the village dogs. I didn't feel afraid. It was not me they were angry with. We got the feuding parties together and there was no further trouble. On another occasion we went out to a prearranged venue by Land Rover where we met the chief and his retinue. He brought horses so we could ride the boundary. The chief allocated me a nice-looking horse. My political messenger stepped in and told the chief to give me a different horse. When we moved off, all of us mounted by this stage, the horse the chief originally allocated me simply took off at a gallop and left its rider hanging upside down by the leg in a peach tree. It could easily have been me. Everyone split their sides laughing at the poor man suspended by one leg.

Constitutional Change

In the early 1960s Lesotho was edging its way towards independence, which was attained in 1966. A constitution had to be drawn up and elections organised and conducted. The fullest possible consultation with chiefs, village heads and the general population was essential. The District Commissioners attended a series of briefing sessions in Maseru and then we went back to our respective districts and organised meetings with local entities at which officers with specialised knowledge attended.

This process, starting with self government, to independence, and culminating in full elections, took four years. The voters' roll was a huge task. District Commissioners were at the centre of things at district level and all the way through the process of getting the country to eventual independence.

Snow Relief

On one occasion I was assigned to a food and fodder relief operation in another district. Oxfam provided funds for a Cessna aircraft and a Bell helicopter. We bagged maize meal for people and lucerne for cattle and with the rear door of the plane taken off we did low runs over suitably flat areas and shovelled the food and fodder off as best we could—I lay on my tummy in the rear compartment and with the door off it was freezing. Where necessary we went back in the helicopter and took food to the remoter villages (Full story page 131). On another occasion we received a message over the crackly police radio that three hundred miners at Letseng la Terae diamond fields, which were located 10,000 feet (3000m) above sea level, were snowed in and starving. Oxfam provided funds to buy food—maize meal, tea, sugar and cooking oil. We commandeered all the police mules and riding horses and managed to get food in. We had to negotiate twenty-two miles of heavy snow between the last point the Land Rovers could reach and where the starving miners in their little thatched huts were located. We had to follow the sharp upper edges of the ridges to get there because the snow was too thick lower down. There were occasions when a mule laden with a hundred kilos of maize meal would sink into the snow up to its tummy and thrash around with no firm foothold. Sometimes it was quite traumatic getting the poor animals onto a firm foothold again.

Some of our men had no sunglasses. By then the clouds had cleared and the sun glare off the snow was dazzling and there were some very sore eyes. The miners were very grateful.

Low Temperatures and Burst Waterpipes

During my first winter in Mokhotlong we had very low temperatures—as low as minus 12C. Water in the galvanised pipes in the hospital and other buildings froze and split the pipes. When temperatures rose and the ice melted, pipes leaked all over the place. The hospital pipes had been laid in the ceiling and the wards were awash. The jeep tracks were totally snowed over and remained so for six weeks. Our only way of getting new pipes in was by air. The air strip was usable but single-engine Cessnas are not well suited for transporting lengths of galvanised piping. We eventually had to get the piping cut at source to lengths which could fit in the Cessna and then be rethreaded. It took some days but we eventually got things under control again.

Road Clearance

The jeep track into Mokhotlong was our lifeline. Every winter it got snowed shut for different lengths of time. We had five long wheel base Land Rovers in Mokhotlong village. Each day at daybreak we would load the Land Rovers up with prisoners and drive an hour to where the blockage started and work at opening the track up. This was at a height of nearly 10,000 feet and it could be very cold. The "tunnel" we dug through the snow to get vehicles through could be five metres deep. It was cold work.

Trying to keep warm on a road-clearing expedition.

A Few Initiatives in Mokhotlong District

Red Cross Baby Clinics

Working with the President of Lesotho Red Cross we established three clinics in remote areas with resident qualified nurses paid by the Red Cross. One clinic was four hours' walk to the nearest jeep track. These clinics were a huge asset to the people in those remote locations.

Sport

Using prison labour we built two good quality tennis courts, a cricket pitch and a nine-hole golf course. The tennis courts were used regularly over weekends and I was a keen participant. We were short of numbers to get up two cricket teams so we got a few prisoners from the gaol to take on fielding duties.

Garden Competition

An annual garden competition for those living in the main village was eventually dropped because the poor judges were subjected to a lot of criticism.

Food for Work

I was the first District Commissioner to set up food for work schemes using maize meal, vegetable oil and beans supplied by the World Food Program of the United Nations. Oxfam provided funds for implements and transport costs. We established village teams of twenty workers (mainly women) who worked five hours a day, five days a week, for three weeks. At the end of three weeks they were paid in food in their village. They built dams and jeep tracks. The scheme was immensely successful and popular. Eventually similar schemes were set up in every district. (Full story page 126)

Village children

Some of the leading citizens of Mokhotlong: trading shop owner, agricultural liaison officer, court official.

Weekly Cinema Show

Mokhotlong village had no electricity. I bought my own 3KVA petrol generator to provide lighting for my house. There was power to spare so we ran a power line to the Courtroom two hundred metres away. It proved adequate to run a small cinema projector which we got through the British Council who also provided weekly films. The hall was packed every Friday.

Distribution of Maize Meal Donated by South Africa

In 1963 while I was DC Mokhotlong, the crops were poor and there were pockets of hunger. The South African government donated maize meal in 100-kilogram hessian bags, but no money for transport. Getting the maize meal up the Sani Pass then distributing it was a major problem. We had to rely on the few jeep tracks we had and animal transport. I arranged a scheme in many areas where payment for transporting the maize meal was not made in money but in maize meal. It worked well. We dealt with 3000 bags.

Ex-Officio Committee Membership

As District Commissioner in Maseru I was a member of the Police Special Branch Security Committee, and for a while on the Housing Allocation Committee and Chairman of the European Primary School Committee. (At that stage I was only just married and without children, so delegated my duties to the Assistant District Commissioner who was married with children.) I am sure I have forgotten some committees. While in this position I also had to attend seemingly endless meetings (not committee meetings) dealing with a variety of subjects.

Entertainment

In Mokhotlong the only hotel burnt down. The result was that Gail and I became the substitute place of abode for official visitors—and others. At that time we had no children and three servants and Gail was an excellent, chatty, welcoming hostess. We accommodated dozens and dozens of people in our ensuite visitor accommodation. For the most part we enjoyed it and so did our guests—though when Gail mistakenly served the Anglican Bishop of Lesotho kerosene instead of sherry, he didn't enjoy it.

Holidays

Leave privileges were generous. Whilst in Mokhotlong we were encouraged to get away and into South Africa for a long weekend every month—to prevent "Mountain Happiness" was the official jargon. There were good hotels within four hours' drive and we had many good times. I was entitled to two weeks a year casual leave and six weeks vacational leave. The vacational leave could be accumulated. Every three years I was entitled to a free boat ticket for myself and family to the UK. Accumulated vacational leave meant that one could be away two and three months on full pay. And so it was being a District Commissioner.

In Power

King Moshoeshoe II

A clever, softly spoken man and very well educated. He married the daughter of a senior Lesotho chief. He was the traditional Paramount Chief by birth. Under the new constitution which was framed on the Westminster system, he lost most of his power to the Parliament and became a constitutional monarch. It must have been hard to accept. At first he objected but ultimately he accepted his new role with dignity.

King Moshoeshoe II
1960

Chief Leabua Jonathan
Prime Minister of Lesotho, 1965-78

Chief Leabua was by birth a minor chief with limited education. It speaks volumes for him that by private reading and study he reached the stage of complete fluency in English and a good knowledge of world and domestic policy. He was very astute and behind the perceived attitude of politeness and moderation there was a man of steely determination.

Chief Leabua Jonathan

I believe Lesotho owes him a huge debt of gratitude for the way in which he handled the very delicate issue of Lesotho / South Africa relations. If a less astute PM had been in power there was a great danger of South African reactions to Lesotho.

See article on Chief Leabua on page 160, and on life before and after the coup. I believe that the coup was ultimately good for Lesotho.

Mountain Trading Store

The horse is very important in Lesotho, particularly in the mountain areas where there are no roads. The Basotho pony is from Arab stock, short and stocky and well suited to rough mountain tracks. My work often took me on horseback over this type of terrain.

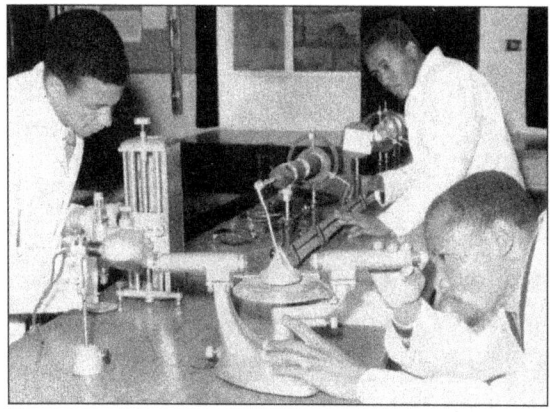

Students at Roma University run by the Roman Catholics. A small university started in the 1960s, it initially offered a limited choice of degrees but expanded into being the main campus for the University of Lesotho, Botswana and Swaziland.

A typical tribal gathering. The multi-coloured blanket is worn like a cloak and serves to keep out the cold, often freezing, weather.
I often found myself involved in this type of "pitso" — gathering of the people.

The missions operate the great majority of the schools and over the years have done a great job in making education accessible to most of the children even in very remote areas. The Government subsidised the costs of operating the schools. As a District Commissioner I was not directly involved in the education system, only if things spilled over into the "political broader administrative" sphere.

Mountain village

This grader was used for both road maintenance and in building contour banks on agricultural land to combat soil erosion.

Soil erosion prevention and dam construction.
It was an offence to plough other than on the contour on sloping land. A farmer could also be charged for not maintaining contour banks.

Stud bulls at a government agricultural centre.

Aerial view of Maseru township, 1960.

Mounted guard of honour, a feature of ceremonial occasions. On June 6 every year we held a ceremonial function in honour of the Queen's Birthday. The ceremonial uniform we wore was designed for tropical climates. June 6 is mid-winter in Lesotho and we often shivered through the ceremony.

Chief Letsie, Minister for Agriculture (left), accepts a gift of a compressor given by the United States Government. I attended the ceremony in my capacity as District Commissioner for the Maseru District.

Lesotho 1960: International Politics in a Changing World

I returned to Lesotho in 1960 to find that a climate of political change had taken place even in the period I had been away. Harold McMillan, Prime Minister of Britain, had made his famous "Winds of Change" speech which predicted the ultimate independence of the British colonies. Immediately after the Second World War (1939-45), India, Pakistan, Sri Lanka and, a while later, Malaysia, had gained their independence. In Africa, the first British colony in the queue was Ghana, headed by Dr Kwame Nkrumah, and then came Nigeria, Kenya, Uganda and Tanzania. With such a rapid progression of independence it followed that a country such as Lesotho must ultimately follow the same course. The apartheid policies which were by now being strongly enforced in South Africa had made it almost impossible for Britain to agree to the incorporation of Lesotho, Bechuanaland and Swaziland into South Africa.

With independence an inevitability, Lesotho found itself moving onto the world scene, out from under the coattails of Britain, with no mineral or industrial wealth and a struggling agriculture. It had just about nothing with which to bargain in its dealings with the rest of the world. But Chief Leabua realised that he did in fact have one quite significant bargaining chip and he used it very astutely. South Africa, because of its apartheid policies, was a pariah in the eyes of most countries and was desperate to improve its image in the eyes of the rest of the world, particularly African countries who refused to have any dealings with South Africa, least of all diplomatic ties.

Chief Leabua set about establishing links with South Africa which fell short of resident diplomatic representation but nonetheless established a line of communication. In return, Lesotho received financial aid, not too obtrusive but very useful. It was a fine balancing act which went far enough to justify in the eyes of South Africa the release of financial aid, but not so far that Chief Leabua could be accused by other African countries of snuggling up to South Africa to the extent that the impression would be given that Lesotho approved of South Africa's policies.

It was financial aid to Lesotho in exchange for at least part diplomatic recognition by Lesotho of South Africa.

At this time China and Russia were actively seeking to project their influence in Africa and were pouring money into support for political parties which would be friendly to them. With the sudden withdrawal of Portugal from the colonial scene, Angola and Mozambique became independent and found themselves ill-prepared to cope with adequate government. The Russians came to their aid and poured money into both former Portuguese colonies and, as a result, their influence was extremely strong. President Julius Nyerere of Tanzania succumbed to offers of finan-cial assistance from China and they built the railway line from Dar es Salaam to the copper belt of Zambia, thus enabling the Zambian government to export their great copper wealth through a port under the control of an African country and not have to continue to rely on their exports going out through South African ports.

The 2000-kilometre railway line was built efficiently and in record time but subsequent management was not good and a lot of the copper continued to be exported through South Africa.

All these events in Africa, particularly in the context of Lesotho, were against a background of tremendous prosperity in South Africa. The mineral wealth of South Africa was immense. The gold price was high and exports in other minerals were strategically important to other parts of the world. At that time, 1960, South Africa produced (in approximate percentages) 70% of the world's gold, 95% of the world's chrome, 85% of the world's manganese, 80% of the world's platinum, 50% of the world's diamonds, and also possessed huge iron ore and coal deposits. Because of the cheap labour, these minerals could be mined at extremely competitive prices and countries such as Japan imported large quantities of coal and iron from South Africa despite the ever-growing hostility towards the country on the basis of its apartheid policies. The strategic metals such as chrome, platinum, manganese and a few others were so important to the economies of the western world that South Africa had no problem at all in finding markets, despite the hostile attitude adopted towards it by both east and west. The South African rand was at that time one of the strongest currencies in the world!

Even when, in the late 1960s, an oil embargo was imposed on South Africa, there was never any great fuel crisis because it always seemed possible to circumvent the embargo. In addition, South Africa with its huge coal resources built facilities for the conversion of coal into petroleum and within a short period was producing 35% of its petroleum requirements from coal extraction.

In the early 1960s there were three main political parties in Lesotho: the Basutoland Congress Party led by Ntsu Mokhehle, the Marema-Tlou Party led by Dr B.M. Khaketla, a journalist and academic, and the Basutoland National Party, led by Chief Leabua Jonathan, a fairly conservative gentleman who the South Africans felt they could do business with.

The Russians gave considerable finance to the Basutoland Congress Party and the Chinese Government to the Marema Party, and the South African Government to the Basutoland National Party. The last thing the South Africans wanted was for Lesotho to become a base right in the centre of South Africa for a hostile African government financed by an even more hostile Russian or Chinese regime. The BCP was quite openly and aggressively anti-government and anti-European and at times quite violent in the way in which it conducted its affairs. The Marema-Tlou Party was more sinister in that it did not openly advocate violence, but one was aware that in an underground sort of way it was planning for change and violence in securing the ultimate outcome. The Basutoland National Party was mainly supported by rural communities and the traditional chieftainship.

When elections were held in Lesotho in 1965, a year before full independence which was achieved in 1966, the South African Government provided substantial financial and discreet material aid to Chief Leabua's Basutoland National Party. I remember a fleet of new Land Rovers suddenly being acquired by the BNP. The South Africans did not publicise this aid in any way. The help given to Chief Leabua by South Africa paid off because he won the election.

On trek in the Mountains of Lesotho

In the 1950s and 60s when I was a District Officer in Lesotho I often had to go on trek in the performance of my duties. The eastern two thirds of Lesotho is very mountainous and travel in this section of the country in those days was very much a question of "in the saddle or on foot". In the 1920s and 30s a network of bridle paths was built and we followed these paths on our mountain trips. Travel in the lowland western section of Lesotho was a lot easier. A road network had been established from the early days of British colonisation dating back to the 1870s. The roads were often rough but they got you there by car. Air services to some mountain centres by small single-engine planes made the difference between one hour in a plane or five days in the saddle. In the 1960s an extensive road-sealing program began which made a big difference.

I was never particularly fond of horses and, unlike many of my colleagues, I never kept a horse of my own, despite the fact that all houses allocated to District Officers such as myself had stables in the back yard. The Lesotho Mounted Police had a large stable of horses and I would obtain my mount from them when an official trek had to be undertaken. A District Officer on trek would travel as follows:

- District Officer (myself)
- Government Interpreter (from District Office staff)
- Political Messenger (from District Office staff)
- 2 police troopers
- 1 pack groom

Each person would have their own horse and our luggage was carried by four mules. I had a small tent for my sole use, a stretcher bed with mattress and never less than six blankets. I cooked on a small kerosene Primus. We normally had to take all our food requirements with us—there were often no reliable shops in the mountain areas to which we went. My travelling colleagues were issued with the equipment they needed from

Government stores. Each of us received a Government travelling allowance from which we paid for our food requirements.

Weather conditions in the mountains varied greatly. The mountain passes reached altitudes of 10,000ft (3000m). In summer the afternoon storms could result in a real drenching. I always tried to have the tents up by 4pm at the latest. On one dramatic occasion we were caught high up on an ironstone plateau in an electrical thunder storm. The flashes of lightning and thunder were simultaneous and constant—like an artillery barrage. It continued for twenty minutes and was very frightening.

In winter there was always the possibility of snow and I was caught quite a few times. The nights could be freezing. It would be not unusual to find the glass of water next to your stretcher bed frozen solid! I often slept cold—the six blankets on top were fine but the cold seemed to creep in from below. I don't know whether appropriate sleeping bags were available in those days. If they were I never owned one.

Snow and thunderstorms were not the only hazards. Flooded rivers could also be a problem. In those days there were very few bridges and major rivers could take days to go down. One had to take advantage of local amenities and on this particular trek we swam the horses across and then got ourselves to the other side in a very leaky boat.

Setting up camp before the afternoon shower of rain. Good grazing for the animals.

Right: Warm sunny weather high up in the mountains with spectacular views made for pleasant riding.

Right: The pimple of a mountain in the background is Thaba Ntlenyane (beautiful little mountain) which is the highest peak in Africa south of the equator (11,500ft). It doesn't look spectacular!

Weather conditions were unpredictable. Falls of snow in mid-summer sometimes occurred. My God!—it could get cold in my tent overnight!

View overlooking the upper reaches of the Orange River. Note the total absence of trees. Not the result of human deforestation: there never were trees.

The local chief gave us a sheep — by tradition we slaughtered it the same day, kept one leg for ourselves and returned the rest to the chief — the local children get their share.

Camped near Orange River which was in flood. Next day we had to get across or abandon our trek.

Swam the horses across. It was not easy to get them to make the plunge. We formed a human half circle, corralled the horses and mules on the river bank in front of us and then slowly advanced, shouting and screaming. Eventually one horse would make the plunge and the others would follow.

After swimming the horses across the river we had to entrust our lives to the local ferryman and his leaky boat. The riverflow was quite fast and we landed on the other side 300 metres downstream. The agricultural officer sitting in the centre could not swim and I could see the whites of his eyes.

Gail accompanied me occasionally on shorter treks. When she remained at home on her own in Mokhotlong for a week or more she was never nervous. I was the only European official resident in the Mokhotlong District with an African population of 50,000. Gail and I were two of the total ten whites in the district. We had four prisoners working permanently in the garden, all of whom would have been sentenced by me. No grudges or resentment ever surfaced.

It was always good to get home again.

Recollections of the Sani Pass in the 1950s and 1960s

My first introduction to the Sani Pass was in 1958, the year I was posted to Mokhotlong as Acting District Commissioner for four months. At this time the Sani Pass was no more than a jeep track, nonetheless it was an important transport corridor for goods coming from Natal in South Africa up to Mokhotlong, which was just starting to develop as a little administrative centre with new buildings such as a two-ward hospital, a little hotel, a new jail and so on. These new buildings were constructed from timber, corrugated iron and cement blocks. At this time all the goods had to be carried up the Sani Pass on the backs of horses and mules—I pitied those poor animals coming up that Pass with 100-kilogram loads on their backs.

The total population of the Mokhotlong District spread over a wide mountain area was about fifty thousand local Basotho people and twenty whites.

It was an exciting place to be a twenty-three-year-old bachelor. Mokhotlong was a genuine outpost of the British Empire. Because of administrative and trade requirements, things were just starting to develop beyond the sleepy colonial era.

The Sani track comes up from Underberg in Natal, from the base of the Drakensberg Mountains to the top of the Pass and, as mentioned earlier, rises three thousand feet in two miles. In those days to get up one could only use a 4WD vehicle. In a long wheel base Land Rover it required twenty-six reverses to get up to the top of the Pass because the corners were so tight.

Vehicles were fitted with a hand throttle thus leaving your feet totally free to use the brakes and the clutch. It was exciting because just over the edge of the road there was a one thousand foot (300m) drop. Sometimes the back of your vehicle would actually be hanging over the edge of the precipice. Big stones had been placed along the edge of the road which lent some sort of assistance to ensure you didn't

Land Rover transporting house furniture up the pass to a destination in the Mokhotlong district.

Bill Bright (left) and John Webb, two directors of Mokhotlong Mountain Transport from mid-1950s to late 1970s. Bill was the business manager and John was the mechanic.

Our 2013 trip up the Sani Pass. From left: Cousin Paul Kirchmann, Ted Nettelton, daughter Beverley and son-in-law, Patrick.

drop over the edge. Some people did. Often the Pass was covered in snow and the corners facing south during winter could be very icy and slippery; this was because in winter during the day the snow would melt then come nightfall the temperature would drop to well below zero and the melted snow would form into ice.

While living at Mokhotlong I normally went down the Pass every few weeks to collect provisions not only for myself but for my staff. The journey of forty-four miles (70km) from Mokhotlong camp to the Sani Pass Hotel at the bottom of the Pass took three and a half hours. I enjoyed the journeys down to the base of the Pass. I had friends who ran a rather precarious transport service up the Pass to Mokhotlong and they lived down in Natal, and we always had a good party at the Sani Pass Hotel or at their houses. All the requirements of the Mokhotlong village, a few commodities and other goods had to be brought up the Pass to stock the trading store in the district. This trading store also bought a lot of wool, which had to be taken down the Pass to Natal and to the market. The trading station sold the basic requirements for the local community such as tinned food, maize meal, sugar, blankets, pots and pans, etc.

At the time that I was in Mokhotlong there was a feud going on between Charles "Makhakhe" Ridgway, the owner of the Mokhotlong store who lived down the Sani Pass in Natal, and Mokhotlong Mountain Transport, the owners of the newly inaugurated Land Rover transport system up the Sani Pass. Makhakhe reckoned that the Sani Pass was made for animals and not for vehicles and refused to use the Mokhotlong Mountain Transport system. All the shop supplies were brought up on pack animals and all the produce was similarly taken down in this way.

When coming up the Pass one frequently had to traverse literally hundreds of pack animals laboriously making their way up, each carrying a load of probably a hundred kilos. The back sores on these animals were often horrendous and it was not unusual to find a dead animal along the track. The journey from the bottom of the Pass through to Mokhotlong took about three days for these animals.

The initial pioneering work to open up the Pass to 4WD transport was done by David Alexander in the early to mid-1950s. It really did require an adventurous spirit and dedication and a belief that it was feasible to develop an economically viable transport service up the Pass

Aerial view of the Sani Pass. In winter there was often snow and ice on the track. Snow skiing took place but the falls were inconsistent. Heavy falls were needed to provide enough snow cover on the ground and to make skiing safe. There were no ski lifts or snow-making machines!

to Mokhotlong and back. A Land Rover that left Natal on its way to Mokhotlong with a full load and was certified roadworthy would never return without mechanical defects. The roads were really very, very rough and often made even more treacherous by ice and snow on sharp inclines. David Alexander was later joined by John Webb, a great mechanic, and thereafter by Bill Bright and Arthur Major. Bill was a fast-talking, good businessman who did a lot to get the financial aspect of the business on track. Their business was one great big adventure. To their credit they developed new types of vehicles and with road improvements they built up a prosperous and successful business.

At the time I was in Mokhotlong a bag of anthracite (coal) cost £3 which in those days was a lot of money. There were no trees in the Mokhotlong district and therefore no firewood so for the local population the main way to cook maize meal—which was their staple diet—was to

Sani track from the top of the Pass. Note its ascent at 3:1 with the road rising 3000ft in two kilometres, and the zig-zag corners. In its early stages of use for 4x4 vehicles there were 23 corners on which the vehicle had to be edged round with up to six reverses per corner — and the track was very narrow with precipitous drops over the edge if the driver miscalculated. At times the Pass was made even more hazardous by ice on the road. We drove using a hand throttle which enabled the right foot to be used for the brake and the left for the clutch.

burn cow patties. It was normal to see people wandering around collecting the dried cow patties. These smouldered hot and produced sufficient heat to cook a pot of maize meal. A cow pat sold for three pence (equivalent these days to 2.5 cents). The local population (other than the civil servants and a few others) lived in round houses with mud walls and thatched roof. Most times they burned a fire in the middle of the hut which became very smoky indeed, so often one saw local people with very red, sore eyes.

In 1962 when I returned to Mokhotlong as District Commissioner, the Sani Pass had been improved greatly, largely due to the efforts of Bob Phillips, Surveyor, who took a special interest in the Sani Pass and Mokhotlong district. By this stage it was possible to drive a short wheel base Land Rover up and down the Pass without any reverses. It was still pretty rough but you didn't have to do those reverses around the corners.

When I was in Mokhotlong in 1958 there was a Basutoland Mounted Police Post at the top of the Sani Pass on the edge of the border between South Africa and Basutoland and when one went through one had to sign a register; there was no need for passports or anything like that. At the bottom of the Pass there was no South African police post, you simply went into South Africa without any sort of official documentation.

In the early 1960s and thereafter things started to change. The political situation became more volatile. Lesotho was seen as a type of refuge for South African black dissidents and the South African Government established police posts all around the borders of Basutoland. This included the Sani Pass, so in going into South Africa you had to carry your passport and there was a well-constructed and adequately staffed South African police post and immigration office at the base of the Pass.

Also, the Mokhotlong Mountain Transport was starting to develop a tourist business and they established a small hotel right on the edge of the escarpment at the top of the Sani Pass. It was an adventure to stay there. It was well furnished and you could keep warm in the evenings on a cold night. There was often snow and the winds right on the edge of the cliff could be freezing. Since those days the tourist business has greatly grown. I haven't seen the Sani Pass Chalet for quite a while but I imagine it would be a well-established tourist centre by now. In our younger days we had some good parties at the Sani Pass Chalet. Gail and I had no children at that stage and so to go out and enjoy yourself at a place like the Chalet was

These two men in their traditional blankets were probably returning from a twelve-month contract in the South African gold mines. The Basuto men had a good reputation and were often the ones chosen for more skilled work. The bright new blankets were probably bought from the two trading stores at the base of the Sani Pass using some of the proceeds of their year of hard work. To walk up the Pass and then to their home villages would have taken them at least two to three days. They are pictured at Stephen Phakisi's store.

a lot less complicated than when our children started to arrive. We ate and drank well to keep the cold out.

From the 1980s onwards, with the development of huge dams in Lesotho with finance from the International Monetary Fund, roads were greatly improved throughout the country and one can now reach Mokhotlong on a sealed road. That is not to say that the Sani Pass itself is sealed but the roads in the district now are a far cry from the way they were fifty years ago when we struggled along jeep tracks in our Land Rovers, taking three hours to cover forty-four miles (70km). I think I preferred the old days. They were exciting.

In the very early days of the Pass when corners were still sharp and hazardous, Mokhotlong Mountain Transport had an African driver called Benjamin. He was an excellent driver and he also had a sense of humour. The worst corner was called Grace's Corner. Where the name came from I know not. But Benjamin, when questioned by tourists, used to say, "By the grace of God I made it around that corner."

In the late 1930s the Police Officer at Mokhotlong was called Hazzy Smith. His wife was a vast woman; they said she could put a bunch of bananas down her front and no one would notice any difference in her body shape. One day she was sitting on the outside dunny at her Mokhotlong home when the seat collapsed and she fell to the bottom of the pit and broke her hip. There were no vehicles in those days and with a broken hip she couldn't sit on a horse, so Hazzy had a litter made. Four men were needed to carry the litter down the Sani Pass which was no more than a goat track, with a three-mile section of the descent at a one in two-and-a-half gradient. They made the forty-four mile journey from Mokhotlong to the road head at the bottom of the Pass in four days.

The Pass has family memories for me in that it was halfway down the descent in my Land Rover when I meet Bill Bright going up. As our vehicles crossed he leaned out and said, "Ted, you have a daughter." I knew Gail was in labour and I was dashing down to Pietermaritzburg to see her. The daughter was Bevie, our first-born. No telephones in those days.

In the early days when the track was very narrow, John Webb, part owner of Mokhotlong Mountain Transport, was driving his Land Rover up the Pass on his way to Mokhotlong one time when he met another vehicle, driven by an African, on its way down. Neither of them was prepared to give way. The outcome was that both spent a chilly night in their respective vehicles facing one another. In the morning they agreed that they would both give ground. Honour was achieved for both and some way or other they were able to pass and each go on their merry way.

Abandoned Car Body at the Top of the Pass: late 1960s

The Pass was very rough and getting a four-wheel-drive vehicle up to the top required a lot of concentration and calm nerves, so getting a two-wheel-drive former London taxi to the top of the pass would have been quite an undertaking.

For many years the abandoned frame of this old vehicle became almost an icon as you got a little beyond the top of the Pass. The story behind this vehicle was that it had been a London taxi and a cockney called Alderskye drove it overland from London and somehow got it up the Pass—I suspect it was almost manhandled up for a good part of the way—then having reached the top the vehicle packed up on him and he abandoned it there. It was not long before the vehicle fell victim to vandals including herdboys who took the tyres to make sandals. The story was that Alderskye, who was quite a character, was in fact snooping around Mokhotlong because there were stories of diamonds being found in the Lesotho mountains, which of course ultimately proved correct and led to the opening of the diamond mine at Letseng la Terae. I am not aware of what ultimately happened to Alderskye or where he went, nor do I know where the old London taxi chassis eventually found a final resting place. The story of Alderskye and his London taxi are part of the early history of the Pass and the Mokhotlong District and I felt it was worth recording.

Remains of 1938 vehicle brought up by a man called Alderskye who was a Cockney from the East End of London in the UK.

Lammergeier — the Bearded Eagle

The lammergeier, often referred to as "the Bearded Eagle", is one of the rarest birds in the world. It can be found in southern Africa right up the African continent and in certain Mediterranean countries.

Picture: Shutterstock

The lammergeier

When we lived in Mokhotlong in the Lesotho mountains a pair of lammergeier for many years mated on the cliffs alongside the Mokhotlong River. My predecessors who had lived in the DC's house in the past spoke of seeing the lammergeier every year but in my time it appeared only rarely.

The lammergeier is allegedly the Bearded Eagle referred to in the First Testament of the Bible.

Lammergeiers near Mokhotlong Village

My house when I was District Commissioner at Mokhotlong from 1962–1965 had a view across the Mokhotlong River to a precipitous rock face on the far side of the river where a pair of lammergeier had nested for many years. I saw lammergeiers only a couple of times in the vicinity of these cliffs but they never actually nested during that period.

Rivers Thompson, who was District Commissioner Mokhotlong in the early 1950s, told me that the birds nested there at that time and he had an almost unbelievable story to tell about a lammergeier chick which fell out of the nest and was raised by a herd boy who looked after it and fed it with lumps of meat and it survived.

When the bird learned to fly it used to go off and come back, then one day—I guess because it was used to humans and was tame—it got too close to a couple of herd boys up the Bafali River who killed it.

The lammergeier is one of the rarest birds in the world and there appear to be no more than a few pairs still nesting in the vicinity of Lesotho and the Drakensberg Mountains. The lammergeier is known to exist right up to Northern Africa and into southern Europe and parts of Western Asia. In the Bible, reference is made to the Bearded Eagle which most probably refers to the lammergeier.

In the Johannesburg *Star* of January 16, 1971, there is an incredible story of three intrepid ornathologists, H.G. Symons, P.R. Barnes and R.O. Pearce, who carried out a quite amazing observation of a nesting pair of lammergeier. Using ropes, they lowered themselves down a sheer precipice to be able to get pictures of the young chick. Over a period of some months they built up a record of a pair of lammergeiers raising this check and also detailed a lot of the habits and behaviours of the bird. A truly amazing feat which will serve the ornithological world in the future as lammergeiers become rarer and rarer.

Animal Transport versus Vehicles on the Sani Pass

The conveyance of goods up the Sani Pass to Mokhotlong village and its surrounds was completely dominated by horses and mules until the mid-1950s when David Alexander started his fledgling 4WD vehicle transport business. David's efforts showed true pioneering tenacity because it was not easy in those early days when the Pass was really not much more that a bridle path, and on gradients of 3:1 the challenge was made even greater.

Mokhotlong Mountain Transport took over from David Alexander in the late 1950s and began to evolve a true vehicular challenge to animal transport. Two trading businesses, "Ridgway & de la Harpe" and "Whitesmith," were long established and profitable and had always relied on animal transport. This was two-way traffic because they had to stock their shops in the Mokhotlong District and then they bought wheat and wool so there was a return load for part of the year bringing that produce to the bottom of the Pass for ultimate distribution to buyers in South Africa. I think it would be accurate to say that everyone was happy with the way things were organised and both the traders and the Basotho animal transport contractors operated in a way in which they could compete and profit. So the introduction of vehicular traffic saw a change in the conduct of buying and selling and there were quite a few who were not comfortable with the established process being faced with competition and change.

From 1962 until 1965 I was full-time District Commissioner for the Mokhotlong District and therefore was well acquainted with what went on in the District. It was then that I first made the acquaintance of Makhakhe Ridgway who was the main partner in Ridgway & de la Harpe and quite a formidable character. He was a big man who had established a well-run business and he was vociferous in his opposition to vehicles starting to operate on the Sani track. He said the track was made for animals not vehicles. On principle he refused to use vehicle transport which inevitably brought him into conflict with Bill Bright of Mokhotlong Mountain Transport. Bill was a fairly brash and outspoken businessman but new to the game and Makhakhe did not take kindly to someone who was prepared to stand up to him.

It was at this stage that I came into conflict with Makhakhe because I felt it was inevitable that vehicular traffic would ultimately dominate transport on the Sani Pass and that improvements to the Pass were bound to occur, which turned out to be the case. I was also aware that the horses and mules, which carried very heavy loads up the Pass and on to Mokhotlong, did suffer severe saddle sores and there was an element of cruelty in it. Makhakhe and I had a number of fairly tense meetings. I remember meeting him on one occasion in his study at his house. He had a tape recorder sitting on the edge of the desk which looked very much like a radio, but I knew it wasn't and that he was obviously recording everything that was being said. I'm sure that in his eyes I was an upstart new DC, still in his early to mid-thirties, while he was a man in his early seventies and, as mentioned, quite a formidable character. I had a very pretty wife and Makhakhe rather liked her because she was completely natural in her dealings with him, unlike all us menfolk.

When things became quite tense he sent a bunch of flowers to Gail and, in a separate parcel to me, a miniature hatchet with a note saying: "Let's bury the hatchet." And that's exactly what happened.

Makhakhe was one of those pioneering Irishmen who made good and who was well respected but who could also be intimidating. Characters like him belong to an era now gone.

The Pack Horse Inn

The Pack Horse Inn was built on a site where there were beautiful views across the Mokhotlong River. In 1958 I remember an English adventurer, by then well into his sixties, who supervised the construction of the hotel, which commenced with his getting cement blocks made in Mokhotlong. These were used for the interior of the hotel. If memory serves me correctly the exterior walls were local stone and the roof was thatched with thatch sourced from wheat hay obtained in the Mokhotlong Valley.

There were eight bedrooms, well set up kitchen facilities, a very nice lounge with great views and a cosy little bar good for a glass of wine on a cold Mokhotlong night. When I returned to Mokhotlong in the period 1962-1965 we used to go to the hotel for an evening drink usually over a weekend and it was quite convivial.

Going back to the sometimes dubious social history of Lesotho, the hotel and bar were not open to non-whites. Incredible when you think back on it; so in the first years it was a whites-only pub, as they all were, rather like South Africa. Up to 1963, local Basotho throughout Lesotho were permitted to obtain a permit from the local District Commissioner which entitled them to buy six bottles of brandy a month. This illogical way of handling the alcohol situation led to many of the African population becoming booze drinkers who would get their six bottles of brandy and proceed to drink every bottle over a short period. The outcome of this was that many Basotho were not accustomed to social drinking and as a result, when the Mokhotlong pub became open to all races we did get our fair share of patrons who did not always behave well; they tended not to sit down and sip a drink but to go in and consume too quickly too many drinks, with the result of bad behaviour. This transition phase was inevitable taking into account the manner in which the alcohol issue had been handled over previous years.

The Pack Horse Inn after a few years started to build up a tourist trade entailing guests brought up by Mokhotlong Mountain Transport or sometimes using their own 4WD vehicles, and they stayed at the hotel. Before the hotel existed there was a government resthouse which was available at a nominal fee but the facilities were pretty basic and it was not used a great deal.

Late in 1963 the hotel burnt down. I remember watching the fire and there was nothing we could do about it as the thatched roof appeared not to have been treated and burnt very freely, and there were no facilities available to turn hoses on to the flames. It was a great loss to the community and thereafter Gail and I found we far more frequently felt compelled to offer accommodation to particularly our official colleagues coming up from Maseru for a few days. We didn't mind, in fact I think Gail quite enjoyed it because she was a very good and generous hostess.

Mountaineers' Chalet

"Capture the mood of Lesotho, (Basutoland) by visiting the Mountaineers' Chalet, the highest licensed hotel in Africa. Meet the friendly Basuto people in their own environment and at the same time enjoy the grandeur of the Drakensberg Mountains.

The Mountaineers' Chalet can be reached from Natal by travelling up the Sani Pass or from the Orange Free State by taking the new trans-Lesotho road from Butha Buthe to the Sani Pass.

Write to Mokhotlong Mountain Transport, Box 12, Himeville for full particulars of this new holiday resort in the mountains."

The burnt-out Pack Horse Inn.

First Date with Gail—1959

The first time Gail and I went out together was in mid-1959. We went to a very nice restaurant in Pretoria accompanied by Roy Davey and his wife—old university friends. It was a good evening tarnished only by the thought that I would be going into hospital next day to have my wisdom teeth out. On the morning of my operation I received a card from Gail which read:

> For want of just a little time
> I have to make my own poor rhyme
> Because I haven't time to buy
> A card to please your jaded eye
> I hope that soon you'll feel quite well
> And that your face will cease to swell
> Thank you again for a lovely evening on Saturday.
>
> *Gail*

Gail with her Austin Healey Sprite.

Gail Franklin Nettelton (nee Turner)
14th December 1934 – 31st May 1996

Gail was born in Pretoria. Her father, Ernest Turner, was a lawyer and her mother, Muriel Turner, came from a wealthy family and never worked to earn her own living at any stage during her life.

Gail lived with her parents at 49 Anderson Street, Brooklyn, Pretoria, an elegant two-storey home which was a wedding present to her parents from her grandfather.

Gail and Beverley.

When I first got to know Gail, she was still living at home but had spent many years away overseas. Gail grew up in the typical privileged South African home with many servants and she went to primary school and high school in Pretoria. She had a good brain but she never used it academically. She left school at the age of sixteen without doing Matric, which was very much the norm for young ladies in those days. After working for a year or so in the British High Commission Office in Pretoria as a stenographer she departed overseas where she soon got herself a job and shared accommodation for a few years with three friends in Earls Court. Those were the halcyon days in London before TV took over our lives. Live theatre was at its zenith and there were all those wonderful galleries and concert halls and so it went on; Gail had many friends and she had a ball.

After some while in the UK she emigrated to Canada. Not that she ever really had any intention of staying permanently in Canada but the Canadian Government was actively recruiting new immigrants and she decided that this would be a good way to get free passage to Canada. She worked mainly in Montreal and then went to Vancouver and after a bit more than a year, she decided that she would go home to South Africa. She caught a bus from Vancouver to New York, boarded the ship and returned to Pretoria. That was early 1959 and at that time I was in Pretoria working as Private Secretary to the British High Commissioner to South Africa. Gail joined the High Commission Office as a stenographer. She was a very pretty girl with a beautiful figure who dressed superbly. I think those fashions of the late 1950s and into the 1960s with the low knee, full skirt and the high stiletto heels were always and still remain my favourite fashion. The girls looked so elegant and they really cared about how they dressed irrespective of what the occasion might be. I think in this modern era people dress over-casually, in fact I think they are pretty sloppy.

Gail and I started going out together in August 1959 and we saw a lot of one another and I got to know her parents. She drove around in a rather elegant canary-yellow Austin Healey Sprite and I had an equally elegant MG Magnet with rosewood panelling and all the trappings. Our courtship went through some fairly bumpy times and I can remember remarking to her that I couldn't understand how such normal parents could produce such an abnormal daughter. However we survived those upheavals and we became engaged on her birthday, 14th December 1960, and were married on 25th March 1961.

I had been transferred back to Basutoland early in 1960 and soon after assumed duty as District Commissioner for Maseru, quite an onerous job. In the lead-up to our wedding I only saw Gail for one weekend in the month because it was impossible for me to get away. Maseru is about four hundred miles, (six hundred kilometres) from Pretoria and in those days only part of the road was sealed. We phoned one another fairly frequently but there was no automatic phone dialling system in Maseru and to get through to Pretoria would sometimes take three hours. Fortunately I knew an African guy who worked on the telephone exchange and he used to try to push my calls through as quickly as possible.

So when we got married Gail and I had really not spent a great deal of time together. A couple of weeks before the wedding I believe she went to her mother and said, "I don't think I want to marry him." It was the usual pre-wedding blues and her mother fortunately said to her, "If you don't marry him, I'm going to disown you."

The wedding was at her parents' house with a big marquee and it was a great occasion; we had lots of friends and we all enjoyed it. We went off on our honeymoon down to the wilderness on the coast of South Africa for two weeks and then it was back to work in Maseru. We lived in a big house in Maseru for about a year before we went overseas. Gail got the house sorted out. She was always a good housekeeper and had excellent taste in decorations and so on. It's worth mentioning that we were looking after this house for people who were on overseas leave and we took over their servants. Old Mary, who must have been in her seventies and almost toothless, was the cook. In the early days Gail wanted to show me how well she cooked. Mary used to sit in the corner and watch her and then a couple of days after we arrived Gail said, "Mary, how do you make gravy?" and so Mary got up, she came across and she said, "Mummy, I was cook at the Hospital for eighteen years. I will show you how to make gravy." After that they got on extremely well. Mary used to tick Gail off when she felt that she was dressing inappropriately. That was the era when skirts were fairly short and Mary used to say to Gail, "Your husband is a big man and you must not walk through the streets with dresses which are so short. It is not good for your husband's reputation." Anyway, Gail used to laugh about it and we did but she was probably quite right.

Ted and Gail married on 25th March 1961.

A visit to Mauritius, 1964. On the verandah of the Curepipe Hotel, Port Louis.

Gail was an enthusiastic member of the Maseru Dramatic Society.

On trek in the Mountains of Lesotho, 1964.

We had a good time in Maseru and it was a great social life. We entertained a lot and made many friends. Gail made friends very easily, she was one of those people who could start up a conversation and laugh and make people feel really at home in no time. She was good company and so she went down really well in Maseru. I can remember one posh black-tie dinner at the Residency in Maseru in honour of the American Secretary of State for African Affairs, and Gail in her mid-twenties was allocated a seat next to the Secretary of State. She wasn't the slightest bit fazed and charmed her way through the dinner.

After about a year I was entitled to a whole lot of overseas leave which I had been storing up. In those days in the Colonial Service I was entitled to a free sea passage from Cape Town to Southampton and back for myself and my family and with my accumulated leave we were entitled to go overseas for four and a half months. We visited about a dozen countries, spent a lot of time with friends in London who gave us free accommodation and all that time I was on full salary. It was great. One of the highlights of course was that we went by sea. Instead of going from Cape Town to Southampton, we were allowed to use the equivalent cost as a contribution towards going on a different route so we went on the old Durban Castle from Durban up the east coast of Africa and eventually got off the ship at Suez. Along the coast our ship, which had one hundred and twenty passengers, had also taken cargo. We would stay for two or three days at each of the ports up the East African coast and we were able to go ashore and often hired a car. We had a wonderful time. There were beautiful beaches and in those days it was still the white man's paradise in Africa. We had a fabulous time—wonderful fresh seafood.

After five months we came back to Basutoland and we were posted to Mokhotlong, right up in the mountains, where there were very mountainous pony jeep tracks and a lot of work on horseback. We had a nice solid stone house and of course there was no such thing as TV, no such thing as telephones. Gail loved it. We entertained a great deal because the hotel burned down so when official guests came up to Mokhotlong, we very often were the hotel. We enjoyed having them and Gail was such a good hostess. We loved it.

After three and a half years in Mokhotlong I was appointed Director of the Basutoland Independence celebrations and we moved down to

Maseru, the capital. By that stage Gail was pregnant (the first pregnancy with Beverley) and she was lucky, she blossomed during pregnancy. A lot of girls get bloated and don't look their best but Gail just bloomed during her pregnancies. We had our adventures during her pregnancy, and Beverley was born about six months before we left the mountains. Beverley would be put into her carry cot in the back of the Land Rover with bags of paraffin and coal and maize meal and flies surrounding her and there would be this little face in the carry cot surrounded by all this stuff. It was a dusty road and she would arrive in Mokhotlong covered in red dust, but it never seemed to worry her. When we moved down to Maseru we were entitled to good housing because I was in fact again a senior person. Gail was, as always, good at making a house feel really inviting and good to stay in. Our final house was a huge place and we enjoyed living there. It overlooked the golf course. We entertained a huge amount. I would say that we went to dinner or drinks or parties about four times a week and our cook Francina did all our babysitting. At that stage Tracy had been born so there were the two girls. Gail loved the social life. We had many dinner parties and she did them so well, and when we went out she was always someone who thoroughly enjoyed mixing; she laughed and made people laugh and it was good.

In 1969 we felt it was time to leave Basutoland. The situation so far as my employment was concerned made it wise to take the big step of leaving because I was a white person with a lot of pressure from up and coming Africans to assume senior positions and I was quite comfortable with that. I think it was just the right time to leave and Gail was happy with it and so we decided that we were coming to Australia. We came across on the old Himalaya and after looking around a lot, we decided that we would live in Adelaide, where we bought the house. Gail once again loved doing up the house and making it feel good and comfortable and so on and for all the time we lived in Adelaide—that would be twenty-five years—she never worked and that was fine with me. She put a great deal of work into the kids and looking after the house and made life very easy for me, and she was happy to do so and we were both comfortable with it.

Gail was a very kind person, a very loving person and she was so good with the kids. Right from the beginning, right through their teenage years and after, if the girls were living at home and they went out to a party

Above: Gail, 1984

Right: Three daughters, 1977 — with Penny, Bev and Tanika.

Right:
Lord Howe Island, 1969 with Bev and Tanika.

and came in at two o'clock in the morning, they would always come and sit on the end of the bed and would have a long chat with Gail all about the goings on of the evening. It was a very warm, intimate relationship between Gail and the children and I guess with me as well. The one thing that she always drummed into the kids was "do your best in life and strive to succeed and be a good person but always remember to respect the feelings of other people."

In our time spent in Adelaide we were very fortunate in that we had a cottage at Coffin Bay for twenty-eight years and it was a great family refuge. One of the golden rules at the cottage was "Thou shalt not disturb a person reading a book." We had the ten commandments on the wall and that was one of them. It was a great family place, you got to know one another again. When I was working hard and the kids were probably working hard at exams and so on, then you would go down to Coffin Bay and as a family you would get together and go out on the boat and get to know one another again, and relax. It was a wonderful place. Then we acquired Wuthering Heights and I guess it all but took over our lives and we loved it. The whole family loved it, the planting of trees and the building of mud-brick houses, and we did it as a family. The kids brought their friends and our friends came along and today I still live at Wuthering Heights. It's a bit of an oasis and I love living here. The big mud brick house—which is now known as Bronte Manor and is a five-bedroom Bed and Breakfast and immensely popular—is an epitaph to Gail. She stood a full five foot two inches (157cm) and those mud bricks weighed about nine kilos each and Gail laid about sixty per cent of them. It's a big house, the sitting room alone is roughly ten metres by six. It's no mean feat getting a brick weighing nine kilos up to a height of 2½ metres as your wall grows higher.

Gail's breast cancer was first diagnosed in 1990. She had surgery and then there was the inevitable post-surgery treatment and she didn't react well. She had a heart attack when they were changing the stem cells and she was accidentally injected with someone else's. She was very lucky to live. Her health was never the same again. She never complained and she carried on for another four years before she died. During that period she did her very best to stay positive which she did very well but towards the end, she just was a very sick person. Gail was a wonderful wife, a wonderful mother and a wonderful person.

Family group — 1980.

Back, left to right: Bev, Penny Ted. Front: Tracy and Gail — 1992.

A Tribute to Gail

In 1960 I was seconded from the British Colonial Service in which I was a District Officer in Lesotho to the British Diplomatic Service where I was assigned to the position of Private Secretary to the British High Commissioner for South Africa. This necessitated my living firstly in Cape Town and then Pretoria. The British High Commission employed a big staff because it covered diplomatic, consular, education and military issues in the relationship between the U.K. and South Africa, and the needs of British citizens living in South Africa.

We necessarily had a big support staff recruited in South Africa— secretarial, lesser finance, chauffeurs etc. I think the secretarial staff (all female) were chosen primarily for their good looks but this is a very derogatory statement to make and I withdraw it.

Miss Gail Turner who recently celebrated her coming-of-age, and will sail next week to spend an 18-months holiday in Europe and Canada. She is the only daughter of Mr. and Mrs. E. J. Turner of Brooklyn. (Photograph by C. A. van Tilburg.)

Gail joined the High Commission staff six months after me. She was then twenty-five years old, very pretty with a beautiful figure, dressed very smartly and smiled and chatted a lot. It was hard not to notice her—I certainly did. On her third day, which was bright and sunny, she arrived at the office in her yellow Austin Healy Sprite with the hood down and wearing a French-style beret— wow! We were married fifteen months later, after which she came to join me in Lesotho. I had by then returned to my District Officer role in Lesotho, which I far preferred to the bitchy diplomatic world.

Thirty countries had at that stage established diplomatic representation in South Africa.

In arranging the seating at a dinner table to seat twelve, how do you determine the senior status between the ambassadors for Uruguay and for Iceland? They were so very status sensitive!

And then back in Lesotho my request to be given the position of District Commissioner Mokhotlong was granted and Gail and I set off for our mountain posting, where our house was nearly 8,000 feet (2400m) above sea level.

Gail admitted she had never once gone on a family countryside picnic yet in Mokhotlong she had to adapt to no telephone, no electricity, no TV, no Austin Healey Sprite cars, no supermarket, no butcher, infrequent visits home, freezing cold winters and then a new-born baby! She took it all in her stride with never a complaint—in fact she loved it. A remarkable woman!

REEDY RIVER
Henry Lawson

Ten miles down Reedy River
A pool of water lies
And all the year it mirrors
The changes to the skies.
Within that pool's broad bosom
Is room for all the stars;
it's bed of sand has drifted
o'er countless rocky bars.

Around the lower edges
There waves a bed of reeds,
where water rates are hidden
and where the wild duck breeds;
and grassy slopes rise gently
to ridges long and low,
where groves of wattle flourish
and native bluebells grow.

Beneath the granite ridges
the eye may just discern
where Rocky Creek emerges
from deep green banks of fern;
and standing tall between them,
the drooping sheoaks cool
the hard, blue-tinted waters
before they reach the pool.

Ten miles down Reedy River
one Sunday afternoon,
I rode with Mary Campbell
to that broad, bright lagoon;
we left our horses grazing
Till shadows climbed the peak,
and strolled beneath the sheoaks
on the banks of Rocky Creek.

Then home along the river
that night we rode a race,
and the moonlight lent a glory
to Mary Campbell's face;
I pleaded for my future
all through that moonlight ride,
until our weary horses
drew closer side by side.

Ten miles from Ryan's Crossing
and five below the peak,
I built a little homestead
on the banks of Reedy Creek;
I cleared the land and fenced it
and ploughed the rich red loam
and my first crop was golden
when I brought Mary home.

Now still down Reedy RIver
The grassy sheoaks sigh,
the waterholes still mirror
the pictures in the sky;
the golden sand is drifting
across the rocky bars
and over all forever
go sun and moon and stars.

But of the hut I builded
there are no traces now
an many rains have levelled
the furrows of my plough;
the glad bright days have vanished,
for sombre branches wave
their wattle blossoms golden
above my Mary's grave.

This poem always makes me think of Gail. I find it very moving.

Life in British Colonial Days
Entertainment, Etiquette and Daily Life

When I first arrived in Lesotho in the early 1950s there remained vestiges of the social conventions typified by the British Raj in India. By the time I left twenty years later, elements of these conventions still survived but they were far more relaxed. As a District Commissioner in the administrative side of government I automatically enjoyed a certain status and was often required to attend formal functions, and Gail and I also did a lot of entertaining ourselves. There were social conventions which one respected and adhered to. I recently was given a book called *Plain Tales from the Raj* by Charles Allen which is about life in India during the era of the British Raj, which lasted for 300 years. I found it fascinating reading because I could in so many ways relate my own life in colonial Lesotho to that described in the book. My own family on the Minchin side (my mother's side) was intimately involved in India in the 18th and 19th centuries. The Cherrys, Minchins and Percivals boasted many senior administrators, lawyers, engineers and in the mid-19th century, four Army Generals (all cousins or father/son), so we can legitimately claim to be very much part of the English regime in India whose social conventions and administrative experiences are described in Allen's book.

The life we lived in Lesotho was very privileged. We had three servants and when I was District Commissioner Mokhotlong, I was entitled to four prisoners to work in my six-acre garden plus a prison warden. For the first few years of marriage we had no children and when we arrived in Australia Gail used to say, "In Lesotho I had three servants and no children, now I have three children and no servants." Francina, our cook, was thoroughly literate and could follow recipes. She was a wonderful cook and made the very best bread which she baked every few days. She also was our nanny and babysitter at night. We had a house maid and a gardener. The house maid was upset when we bought a washing machine because she thought she was going to lose her job—she learnt to use the washing machine and kept her job! John Nking, the gardener, had a history of drinking and when he first arrived his eyes looked like poached eggs. I took him on after issuing an ultimatum and for the next eight years he was a most loyal and reliable worker. He cleaned my car every week day before I went to work (he had Saturday and Sunday off) and looked after the garden well, apart from losing a few toe nails to the lawnmower!

Francina had Saturday afternoon to Monday morning off. Otherwise, she worked a full day serving all three meals and doing all the washing up. When one of the children was playing up she would strap them to her back in a blanket and continue her work. The children loved it and usually fell asleep in no time. The relationship with our servants was almost feudal. We fed them, we housed them, we paid for their medical needs, we clothed them and they received a small monthly wage. Francina's three children lived with her in her rooms on our property. It was a relationship of mutual respect. I can recall an incident which Beverley, then three years old, has never forgotten. Francina usually fed the girls their breakfast in the kitchen and on this occasion Beverley was being a little cheeky madam. When Francina put Beverley's egg and soldiers on the table in front of her and Beverley didn't say thank you, Francina said to her, "Beverley you can go outside and find your manners and then come back." Beverley obediently went outside and remembers wandering through the garden calling, "Manners, where are you, manners?" as she looked behind trees and bushes. She never forgot this disciplinary lesson.

Gail and Francina had an excellent rapport. Both had very young children. I recall the birth of Francina's third child. We had a big cocktail party at our house that night and Francina was handing trays of snacks round. Halfway through the evening she disappeared to the kitchen and when Gail went to see what the problem was, she found her sitting on a chair in labour. John Thiselton Dyer and I carried her hastily to the car. Her waters broke as we crossed the lawn and I remember her saying, "I am finished." We got her to the hospital just in time. The baby was fully delivered within ten minutes of her arrival. Our children and Francina's often played together but there was a well-defined social bar in the white community which meant that outside one's own premises there was little mixing between the children of the white elite and those of the local black community. In the capital, Maseru, there was a school for white children only. These colour/social barriers were steadily eroded from the early 1960s onwards and by the time I left Lesotho in 1969 the situation was one of quite a bit of inter-mixing.

In the 1950s the hotels and clubs in colonial Lesotho were for whites only. There was a permit system for hard liquor for black males. As District Commissioner, my office was responsible for the issue of these permits. The permit allowed the holder to buy six bottles of hard liquor a month from the hotel bottle shop. The bottle shops, all white-owned, made a fortune. The permit system had adverse effects because it tended to encourage binge drinking and when the hotels and clubs were eventually opened up to the whole population, white and black, the well-trained binge drinkers were a problem in the previously well ordered social atmosphere of the hotel bar. The outcome was that most white people deserted the public bars and drank socially at home or amongst their friends. Throughout the 1950s the Maseru Club played an important role in the social life of a great number of the white community. The Club had a dance hall, big bar, tennis courts, squash courts, cricket oval, bowling green, swimming pool, golf course etc. There was an active drama group which periodically put on excellent plays. Long dress and black tie dances were held on the usual festive occasions and a social gathering in the bar was normal after cricket or tennis or polo or whatever. We all did our few days behind the bar. Gail and I enjoyed many a happy occasion in the Club.

Gail participated in the drama society and proved herself to be a talented actor. I was a very keen golfer, cricketer, rugby and squash player and because all these sports were centred at the Club, I spent many a happy time in its precincts.

The first admission of a black person to the Club in the late 1950s is an event worth mentioning. Dr Aaron ("A.D.") Lebona was a respected doctor and a good golfer. After the white community had had a chance to look him over, it was decided that in the light of political events which were inevitably going to lead to independence for Lesotho, it would be opportune to admit a black member within the previously exclusively white walls of the Club. Dr Lebona was well accepted. He was such a nice man, ideal as a first step towards breaking down the social barriers. Dr Lebona played golf regularly and after a while he was joined by a number of black club members.

I remember playing golf with Dr Lebona in a tournament where a number of the players were whites from across the border in apartheid South Africa. Two of our foursome were Afrikaner farmers who had known nothing other than the rigid black/white social system of South Africa as it was then. To find themselves playing golf on equal terms with a black man would have been a traumatic experience for these two Afrikaners. Dr Lebona was his normal pleasant self, not at all fazed by the situation—and he played better golf than them. I remember hearing one Afrikaner saying to the other, "Maar hy is goeie ____" and then using a very derogatory word for a black person. This means, "My word, he is a pretty good ____." The term used is a very derogatory one but the Afrikaner in this context would have used it not in a derogatory sense but because that was the way he had always spoken. After golf the two Afrikaners had a social drink with Dr Lebona!

At dinner parties we were always aware of the conventions attached to seating at the table. Sometimes it was difficult to decide who the most senior couple were to be seated on the right of the host and hostess respectively. At formal dinner parties it was normal for the ladies to get up from the table and leave the men to have a glass of port on their own. I enjoyed the little all-male chit chat before we joined the ladies. It gave the ladies a chance to powder their noses and visit the toilet if they wished to do so. The men often went outside to visit the lawn! In the dry winter the lawn often had green patches dotted around!

In the early 1960s as local Africans started to take over some senior positions, it became almost an unwritten convention that you would include a sprinkling of black guests at your cocktail parties. The wives of some black senior office bearers found it difficult and it was not always easy to engage in conversation. It was interesting the way the situation played itself out. After a few years it was as if everyone realised that the barriers had been broken down and it became quite acceptable for you to choose your friends whether black or white and entertain as you felt comfortable. Of course there were still those official functions where protocol determined who would attend but these became far more relaxed because black and white had gone through that barrier together and knew one another better, and the atmosphere was so much easier.

Mary: Our First Housemaid

After our honeymoon, which would have been in mid-April 1961, we moved on to Maseru. I resumed my duties as District Commissioner Maseru, and we moved into a double-storey house which had been vacated by a Mr and Mrs Jarvis who had gone on four months' overseas leave. We also inherited their servants and that was quite a little episode.

The cook-come-maid was quite a formidable person and had difficulty in accepting that Gail, who stood a full 5'2", was very pretty and was in her mid-twenties, was the mistress of the house. After a very short time she wisely abdicated her position to her mother who was a toothless granny but a great character. Her name was Mary. Gail recalls that for the first few days Mary sat in the corner of the kitchen and watched Gail preparing the meals until one day when Gail was struggling to make gravy, she asked "Mary, how do you make gravy?" and she got up and said "Mummy, I was cook at the Hospital for eighteen years. Let me show you." She always called Gail "Mummy" which is really a term of endearment. After that things went swimmingly in the house because Gail and old Mary established a real bond and got on in their own way extremely well.

I well recall an occasion when we were going out to a cocktail party and Gail came down the stairs in a knee-length dress and Mary took

Mary, our first housemaid in Lesotho — what a character!

up a position at the foot of the stairs with her hands on her hips and she said, "You are married to a big man. You cannot go out with a big man wearing a short dress like that." It was quite an occasion because I had to explain to Mary that I accepted the dress that Gail was wearing and that that was the fashion amongst the white people and that they would not regard it as flaunting herself in some sort of seductive way.

I also recall an occasion on a Sunday afternoon when Mary came home—she had sleeping quarters at the rear of the house—and she had an old broken umbrella and had obviously been to a party because she was so very happy and with that toothless grin and waving that umbrella, she said, "And it is a very happy day". It was really very funny because she was a funny person and a very lovable person.

John Nking, our gardener.

It was at this time that we took on John Nking as our gardener. He had eyes like poached eggs from drinking too much. However, he was basically a good man and I found he was a good worker but it was essential to let him go off on Saturday morning for the full weekend because then he met up with his friends and obviously spent the weekend drinking. However, he would be back Monday morning, polishing and dusting my car before I left for work as he did every single morning of the week. I would give instructions about planting and watering and weeding in the garden and he carried out those instructions well. John stayed with us for the rest of our time in Lesotho and, the drunken old so and so, he served us well.

Gail and I both greatly enjoyed those colonial days. I do not have any regrets about the time I spent in the Colonial Service. I feel I can take pride in the fact that I never in my eighteen years in Lesotho had a racial accusation directed towards me and the fact that the newly installed Prime Minister, Chief Leabua Jonathan, asked me to be his secretary must carry

Francina with Tanika on her back.

some meaning as to my standing in the eyes of many Basotho.

When I left Lesotho, we—the British Administration—left a reasonably well functioning administration, hospitals, courts, police etc. Literacy, which was largely in the hands of the Missions, stood at 90 per cent. I was proud, not embarrassed, by what we left behind. Fifty years later it is such a mess not only in Lesotho, but in most parts of Africa. The colonisation of Africa certainly had its downside, but on the other hand in British colonies we established an orderly government structure. I do not accept that the failures of so many countries in Africa is solely attributable to colonisation. Much of the problem comes from the greed and demagogic attitude of many African leaders. Colonisation is all too often used as an excuse for failure. After all, most former colonies have had many decades to sort out the so-called "colonial legacy".

The Wax Candle Factory

I recall accompanying the Prime Minister in 1967 to the opening of the first factory in Lesotho, the Wax Candle factory in the Leribe district. It employed one person but I guess it was a start though one has to chuckle at the fact that the Prime Minister of a country would agree to take the lead in a ceremony to celebrate the opening of a factory which employed one person. But Chief Jonathan always believed that there was an industrial future for the area. In the end he was right in the fact that Lesotho has a system of commercial land ownership with foreigners not permitted to gain freehold title to land, only long-term lease which was a strong disincentive to prospective investors.

This restriction persisted for many years and investment was further discouraged by political instability. The United States in the 1990s brought in the African Growth and Activities Act which gave African countries access to the US garment industry with reduced tariffs. Foreign firms took advantage of this Act and set up factories in Lesotho. By 2008 Lesotho's export of textiles to the US totalled $340 million per annum and employed 40,000 workers in forty countries. Wages averaged $420 a month; compare this to Bangladesh. Trade unions were allowed and the workers are not exploited.

Land Ownership in Lesotho

Lesotho has a system of communal land ownership. From the time of the arrival of Europeans in the area which is now Lesotho in the 1860s, Chief Moshoeshoe in his wisdom made it clear that the Europeans would never be allowed to own land in Lesotho. The story goes like this: In the 1860s Chief Moshoeshoe invited the Paris Evangelical Mission Society to Lesotho where they would be free to work amongst the people and erect their churches and other buildings but they would never be granted free title of the land on which their buildings were erected. But there was also the request that they teach his people to read and write. The French Protestants were followed by the Roman Catholics and the Church of England. These three religious denominations can be very proud of their achievements in education and the fact that they were prepared to establish a network of schools not only in the easily accessible lowland area but also in remote mountain areas. Lesotho boasts the highest literacy rate of any country in Africa with 94 per cent of adult women able to read and write and 86 per cent of males.

The same system of land ownership persists today. Trading businesses have operated on land leased to them many decades before and there have been no big problems. This land system did act as a deterrent to big foreign businesses setting up factories in Lesotho, but this problem appears to have been overcome and Lesotho by 2010 was the biggest textile manufacturer in Africa, with the bulk of the exports taking advantage of a United States policy brought in in the 1990s (the African Growth and Activities Act) giving preference to textile imports from African countries at reduced tariffs. Foreign firms took advantage of this Act and set up factories in Lesotho.

Trout Fishing in Lesotho

Trout were introduced into the mountain streams of Lesotho in various locations in the 1930s and they flourished. Previously the rivers contained only yellow fish, a very bony fish which moved downstream and out of Lesotho in winter. The Basotho people rather surprisingly were not interested in the indigenous yellow fish and they appear never to have been part of their diet.

The British were very particular about trout fishing being conducted in accordance with the rules of sportsmanship as practised in the United Kingdom and a special proclamation was gazetted thus making "doing the right thing" legally enforceable. Spinners, baited hooks and nets were outlawed. Imagine the outrage when a Roman Catholic brother from a remote mountain mission in the Mokhotlong district where I was stationed was reported to be dynamiting mountain river pools in order to gather trout to feed the boarders at the mission school. To some it was worse than

I spent a lot of time up to my knees in the water fishing downstream.

dropping an atomic bomb on Hiroshima! I got him to report at my office and cautioned him not to do it again—he should rather ask the Pope for a fishing rod with trout fly and tackle!

The trout were both rainbow and brown by species. The rainbow seemed to flourish in the fast-flowing streams whereas the brown preferred quite deep pools. Some enormous brown trout were caught occasionally, over five pounds. I preferred fishing for rainbow trout because they are a magnificent fighting fish which jump out of the water and battle the line to the end. I prefer trout fishing to ordinary fishing because one is playing the line and doing something all the time—never just sitting there with baited hook waiting for something to happen.

David Alexander's book *Sani Pass: Riding the Dragon,* written in the mid-1950s, describes the type of trout fishing we enjoyed on our doorstep when I was District Commissioner Mokhotlong in the 1960s. We stuck to the rules of trout fishing so important to English gentry but in many respects it was quite rugged—but a lot of fun. We caught many delicious rainbow trout, some of them so brave the way they fought that one sometimes returned them to the water.

Fishing for trout on the Mokhotlong River, 1963. We caught mainly rainbow trout. In the fast-flowing water they put up a tremendous fight, jumping right out of the water many times. They were mainly about half-pounders and great eating.

Alan Savory, a noted English author, enquired one year about trout fishing in the mountains and, being a keen fisherman myself, a trout fishing expedition appealed to me. My fishing tackle was rudimentary: a few flies—a yellow-brown monstrosity nearly the size of a dragonfly that John Kirkman had tied for me was my favourite—no net or waders or any fancy gear. Alan must have thought me pretty green, yet I usually caught as many fish as the others.

Alan wrote a story for the well-known British publication *Country Life* about his visit to Mokhotlong. In part, he said:

"There were patches of land in the Mokhotlong Valley bordering the river planted with a thin cropping of mealies where gangs of women were hoeing. In many places the grass was thin and overgrazed and in this bleak and utterly remote land, where beauty and starvation go hand in hand, the greatest crime is stock thieving. The Basuto are also bedevilled by ritual murders that strike fear and dismay into every family.

"The fishing potential of Basutoland is enormous. The streams are rocky, fast and wild with waterfalls; they have slow, deep reaches and quick torrents of foaming water that glide as clear as crystal over beds of round stones. There are Rainbow and brown trout of fighting size, but there are not enough of them and the streams badly want restocking. Alexander and I had good fishing, but there were long stretches of clear water without life of any kind, other than a few yellow fish.

"There is some fabulous fishing in a stream that rushes down some far mountain-side into one of the distant gorges, but one can get to it only by plane and the air is a little thin for a light aeroplane to land on the available space. One man made the flight, however, and caught a score of two-pounders before the pilot dragged him back to the plane so that they could take off while there was still light among the peaks.

"We fished all day with varying success, but the country was so utterly wild and lonely that the sport was almost of secondary importance, range after range of mountain peaks and green hills and gorges and streams; a wild and lonely land washed by huge fleets of clouds that sail over for ever from beyond the hills across the horizon.

"We watched the plane come in from Maseru, which it does four times a week, but when it had gone it was no more than a passing thought.

"The world was of high hills, mealie fields and tumbling, rushing streams, of Basuto men and women in coloured blankets and naked children playing in the dust, of stone huts and the acrid smell of burning cow dung. There were long trails reaching away over the hills, views of distant riders vanishing in the blue haze, the sharp outlines of peaks against the glare of the sky at mid-day, of vultures slowly circling; there were the gathering clouds of evening, as the peaks turned red as blood with the last rays of the sun, and then dark as death as smoke from the huts rose in the blue spirals in the last of the evening light."

Fishing a deep pool at Onbow in northern Lesotho.

Some weekends we (usually Gail and I) would go out with a fly rod (and Gail with a book) and work our way along a mountain stream. By lunchtime we would have a few half-pound trout and these we gutted and
wrapped in tin foil with a bit of butter and put them on the fire for a short while. They were delicious. Nothing better than a freshly caught fish.

Right:
The local herd boys were always interested onlookers but they never showed any desire to fish for themselves.

Right:
A swim at the end of the day was always refreshing.

The Maletsunyane falls high up in the mountains. It was possible to get to the base of the falls, where there were good trout pools, by way of a precipitous rocky path. I took the Australian High Commissioner to South Africa fishing at this spot—a really nice man but no fisherman. He never ventured into the gorge—he stayed up top and drank beer all day.

Fishing in the Mountain Streams of Mokhotlong

Before the arrival of British colonial fishing buffs, the rivers of Basutoland were home to only one indigenous fish, the yellow fish, which could grow to a good size (three pounds) but were difficult eating because of the bones. They remind me of the European carp both in appearance and eating qualities. My introduction to yellow fish was by Dr Bertha Hardegger at a remote Roman Catholic Mission at Thaba Iseka. She came upon me doing some fishing (she was on horseback, so was I) and she invited me to dinner that night. The meal was yellow fish, full of bones and eaten by candlelight (no electricity). I really struggled; she chewed up the bones and swallowed them! A tough lady!

The law to regulate trout fishing by persons of European origin only controlled trout fishing, and baited hooks could still be used to catch yellow fish. Very few Basuto fished the rivers which I found surprising as the indigenous fish were abundant. In so many parts of the world where there is a subsistence economy people make full use of the local fish resources.

In the period that Gail and I lived in Mokhotlong we did a lot of entertaining and were often able to serve fresh trout at our dinner table. At certain times of the year we had wonderful asparagus and after good rains, wild mushrooms as big as soup plates were abundant. When all three delicacies coincided, which was not infrequent in spring, we dined in true gourmet fashion. In most rivers the trout were fat and succulent, usually about half a pound and excellent eating. However, in the more remote upper reaches of rivers such as the Senqunyane the water was overstocked and the fish had big heads and small bodies. In these areas it would not be unusual to catch forty fish in a morning.

An Adventurous Afternoon in Snake Country

At Mokhotlong we were surrounded by very mountainous terrain. There were many fast-running streams ideal for trout. The roads were no more than jeep tracks suitable for four-wheel-drive vehicles only. One Sunday afternoon I hopped into my Land Rover with my fishing rod and drove for an hour up to the Mokhotlong River following a very rough track. This took me into remote cattle post (farm) country, no habitation, no people, just a few cattle, sheep and goats.

Rinkhals cobra

The track was at least 200 feet (about 60 metres) above the river but I could see the stream below clearly. Eventually I picked out a series of pools which looked as though they might be favoured by trout so I parked my vehicle and made my way down what turned out to be quite a precipitous descent to the stream below. My hopes of finding fish in the pools were fulfilled and in a short while I pulled in two fat ¾-pound rainbow trout—my mouth watered when I thought of the delicious evening meal to come: nothing nicer than a freshly caught rainbow trout. There is something extra good about trout because it has no scales to be rubbed off, just that smooth outer skin.

Having taken two beautiful fish out of the first pool, I decided to move downstream to the next. I wore shorts and shirt, no socks and a pair of lightweight sandshoes suitable for walking. I had walked a short distance when in the corner of my eye I picked up movement and when I glanced down, there alongside my bare leg was a big ringkhals (cobra) with head raised and hood spread out, which denotes aggression. Its head was no more than six inches from my leg, in easy striking distance. Why it had not bitten me has always been a mystery to me. In my alarm I moved away fast and then proceeded to stone the snake to death—a totally needless reaction which I am not proud of. Anyway I decided I still needed a few more fish to take home and moved downstream to the next pool where I caught two more fish. I wandered across the stream and began to walk further downstream to a third pool that looked promising. As I walked, in the corner of my eye once again I caught a movement and there alongside my leg was another ringkhals snake as big and fat as the first one and with head raised, hood spread and in a perfect position to sink its poisonous fangs into my leg. This time I took off at full pace and made straight up the steep slope and back to the Land Rover. If I had been bitten I truly believe I would not have survived. There was no one around to help me, I had told no one which pools I intended to fish and there would have been a dozen to choose from.

When bitten by a snake the first rule is not to engage in strenuous exercise. I would have had no option other than to make my way up the slope to the Land Rover—a very strenuous exercise. Then I would still have had an hour's drive back over a track full of dangerous narrow sections alongside steep drops to the river below. I was indeed very lucky that afternoon.

Stephen Phakisi

Stephen Phakisi was a Mosotho shop owner who had a business not far from Mokhotlong on the Bafali River. Over the years, I often fished the Bafali stream. It had good trout pools. Stephen used to go to church on a Sunday morning in Mokhotlong and he often stopped for a chat. He spoke good English. We got on well but to my surprise most of my DC predecessors spoke of him as a "won't listen" trouble-maker. After I left Mokhotlong he built a shop alongside the Mokhotlong airstrip.

Stephen Phakisi

Two well-dressed customers at Stephen's store.

Stephen Phakisi built this structure on the edge of the Mokhotlong airstrip about 1975.

MORE than 7,000 feet above sea level, in the rugged hills of Lesotho, stands this sign of modernity. It is at the tiny aerodrome at Mokhotlong — population about 200. The block of buildings which dominate the aerodrome and is second to the Government offices in size, carries the legend "Tourism is a giant industry — use Lesotho Airways." This picture was taken when a "Mercury" reporter went there last week.

Air Travel in Basutoland

Basutair

The air service into Mokhotlong was vital. Basutair flew from Maseru (the capital of Basutoland situated in the lowlands) into Mokhotlong five days a week bringing the post, passengers and urgent items that could fit into planes. When I first worked in Mokhotlong in 1958, Basutair operated a fleet of three Tri-Pacers. They were painted blue and could carry three passengers plus a bit of luggage. The flight from Maseru to Mokhotlong took about an hour and encountered the Maluti Mountains with peaks up to 10,000 feet high. There was in those days no road from Maseru to Mokhotlong and the only alternative to flying was to ride, which took a minimum of five days. The airstrip at Mokhotlong was six hundred and fifty yards (600m) long. My chicken coop was the fuselage of a DC2, testimony to aviation exploits that went wrong in earlier years.

Piper Tri-Pacer built mid-1950s. Basutair had four of these planes. They peformed remarkably well at altitudes of 10,000 feet. When stationed at Mokhotlong, I had the choice of travelling one hour in a Tri-Pacer or five days on a horse to get to Maseru, the capital.

This fuselage of an aircraft damaged on the Mokhotlong air strip was brought down to Himeville on a platform built on top of a vehicle.

Basutair upgraded its planes over the years and operated six-seater Dorniers by the late 1970s. Dick Southworth was the pioneer who really got the airline going. It was his determination and skills as a pilot that made it happen. He was a dedicated fly fisherman and always had a rod in the plane. There were some great trout streams in the mountain areas to which he flew. In about 1960 during a fishing expedition at Semonkong, his trout fly lodged in his eyeball. He was on his own and unable to fly the plane, spending a very painful night on the airstrip until a plane came up to fetch him. His eye was damaged and he did not get his commercial licence back for five years.

One of the Basutair pilots was a great ladies' man—he had a very beautiful wife and two young children but this did not deter him from chancing his luck with pretty passengers. I remember one occasion when he had a very pretty unmarried English girl as a passenger. The plane predictably developed "engine trouble" and was able to land in a paddock on the South African side of the border conveniently close to a hotel. The plane was able to take off next morning after the pilot fiddled around with it. The "goings on" in the hotel overnight are left to the imagination but the pilot and the English girl seemed well pleased.

In 1958 I was flying out of Mokhotlong to Maseru where I was to catch a plane to London on overseas leave. We were flying between the jagged peaks of the Maluti Mountains when the engine of the plane stopped (single-engine plane). There we were drifting over the jagged peaks with no hope of a suitable place to make an emergency landing. The pilot looked at me and said, "What do we do now?" I said, "You're the bloody pilot, you tell me." He looked blank and perplexed and then with a laugh said, "Oh, I forgot to switch over to the other petrol tank."

In the late 1950s a Basutair Tri-Pacer made an emergency landing in a maize field in a mountain valley and sustained a fair bit of damage. The pilot broke his ankle. One of the passengers was an old Mosotho lady. Before mak-ing the emergency landing there was much talk between the pilot and his other passenger as to where they could come down.

Snowbound area from the air.

Cessna weather-bound in Mokhotlong just outside our fence. We often accommodated stranded pilots and passengers.

When the plane eventually came to a stop quite badly damaged, the old Mosotho lady, quite unperturbed, proceeded to remonstrate with the pilot nursing a broken ankle because she had paid him a lot of money to take her to Maseru town, not to dump her in a maize field in an area she did not recognise!

In 1972 there were riots, motivated by the political opposition, in a mountain area where there were many African diamond diggings. To quell the riots the then Commissioner of Police commandeered two small planes, took the luggage doors off, put a policeman in the back of each plane, each with a bag of hand grenades. The planes flew over the riotous mob and dropped hand grenades on them. About a hundred rioting miners were killed.

Helicopters were often used for mineral exploration.

Cessna on Mokhotlong Airstrip. The pilot's seat came off its hinges as he was taking off.

Drakensberg Air

In the 1960s Drakensberg Air flew twin-engine Dornier biplanes from Ladysmith in Natal to Mokhotlong. These old planes were from the wood and paper machines era, but performed surprisingly well. One pilot reckoned he remained safe so long as the woodworm kept holding hands!

They mainly flew out mine recruits going to the gold mines. When Gail was pregnant with Bevie and her parents were living in Hilton, Natal, we kept a car at Ladysmith airport and Gail would fly down to Ladysmith once a month, pick up her car and drive down to stay with her parents and have a monthly medical check-up. Gail did not want her check-up with the Mokhotlong doctor, who was a drug addict.

On one such flight when Gail was seven months' pregnant the pilot, who was not experienced, came over the mountain escarpment and found himself with a solid cloud mass below. He couldn't find a gap in the cloud to get down and in hilly country you can't afford to take a chance that you will find flat ground below if you fly blind through the cloud mass. The pilot panicked and they were eventually over the ocean near Durban but he refused to make radio contact for fear that he would lose his pilot's licence if the authorities knew what he had done. The pilot turned back over land and Gail said they found one small gap in the cloud and came down to land in a cow paddock. The plane was not pressurised and the doctor was concerned that Gail had gone to an altitude of over 10,000 feet (3000m) when seven months' pregnant. It had no ill effects on Gail or the unborn Beverley.

Two-engine Dornier biplane which performed very well in the mountains at high altitude.

Flying Doctor Service

The flying doctor service commenced in the early 1960s. The doctors and pilots had to be adventurers to take on the job. The airstrips were hazardous in the extreme. I flew with them once and it was an experience I declined to repeat. However, they provided a service which greatly benefited people in the mountains where medical services were few and far between.

Dr Geoff Goodyear. The airstrips the Flying Doctors had to land on were sometimes hair-raising.

AIRBORNE DELIVERY FOR A BABY

DR. GEOFF GOODYEAR, of the Flying Doctor Service, of Lesotho, is another man who braves the sometimes terrifying mountains of Lesotho to bring medical care and comfort to the people attending the six clinics in the remote highlands.

He has the unique distinction of having delivered a baby in a single-engined aircraft high above the mountains.

"The mother had been in labour for three days and I had been unable to get through to the nearby clinic because of the weather. Nothing for it but to sit her on a horse and take her to the plane in which we would fly her to a hospital in Maseru.

THE TRICK

"After being airborne five minutes the baby started to arrive. Sitting on that bouncing horse had done the trick. Imagine delivering a baby in a light plane — it's quite different to a spacious ward.

"Operation over, we landed on the strip and delivered mother and baby to the clinic. You should have seen the faces of the nurses."

The mother and baby went home the next day probably on horseback.

The only charge for the flying doctor is 20 cents for drugs or injections. The Basotho believe that injections are more effective than medicine because they have some similarity to the skin cutting by their witchdoctors.

Every morning Dr. Goodyear takes off in the bitterly cold dawn to be dropped at one of the clinics. He is picked up late in the afternoon if the flying conditions allow it, otherwise he stays over in one of the hut clinics.

ARE RISKS

Dr. Goodyear would like to see the flying doctor service expanded—these small-boned women need more pre-natal and post-natal care. Another thing he feels strongly about is that there should be more preventive inoculations.

Obviously there are risks in flying over these mountains and Dr. Goodyear, a volunteer in the International Volunteer Service, accepts them.

The landing strips are basic stretches of reasonably level ground on which there are such hazards as cows, sheep and horses.

One doctor acting as locum for one of the mission doctors was killed in an air crash recently.

Said Dr. Goodyear: "If your people on the other side would like to help us, we would be grateful for clothing; it's perishing cold up there for the Basotho."

Food for Work

In 1964 when I was District Commissioner Mokhotlong, I made a successful submission to the World Food Program for assistance to start a "food for work" program. We built many roads and dams. The scheme was based on the concept of village labour (male and female) doing the construction work. A worker was required to work five hours for five days for three weeks, then received an agreed payment of maize meal, cooking oil, beans and dried milk. The food was handed to the worker "on site". It was a popular and successful scheme. The biggest problem was providing adequate funding in a cash-strapped country to enable the roads to be maintained in a reasonable and usable state of repair after they had been built. The scheme built many roads in the mountains, and also stock watering dams.

The other project to which the Food for Work program gave considerable support was helping transport the Mokhotlong share of the South African grain gift, which amounted to 300 bags, up the Sani Pass jeep track to Mokhotlong. We had no cash to pay for transport so we devised a scheme whereby any grain brought up the Pass by pack animals was paid for in grain—one bag for every two brought up on an animal. It worked well.

Road survey work was not always easy.

The Land Rovers endured rough treatment.

Village work gang.

JONATHAN ON VISIT TO FOOD PROJECTS

The Friend Correspondent

MASERU

THE PRIME MINISTER of Lesotho, Chief Leabua Jonathan, will visit the rugged and scenically beautiful Quthing and Qachasnek districts today and tomorrow to inspect food-for-work projects.

He will be accompanied by Mr Ted Nettle, director of the food aid programme which is responsible for the projects.

A Government spokesman said yesterday that the Prime Minister would spend much of the time in the southern districts looking at self-help road projects.

One of the most prominent features of the road projects in the south is the completion of the road between Qachasnek and Quthing. Travellers can now travel by Jeep between the two towns without having to travel through the North-Eastern Cape as has been the case previously.

There is a seven-mile section of road along the Quthing River Valley which cuts out a very steep climb and dips from Mount Moorosi to Devil's Staircase Peak.

The Friend 25 September 1968

Right: Pick and shovel work. The ladies of the village build a new road.

Right: A hundred picks can overcome a rocky obstacle!

Below: Jeep track through the snow.

This dog seemed not to be worried by the cold and snow.

Save the Children Fund

This Food for Work program was expanded to include the Save The Children Fund school-feeding scheme. By the late 1960s a scheme was operating which fed one hundred thousand children lunch every school day. The children received maize meal, soya oil, dried milk and sometimes beans. Under a separately funded scheme, school kitchens were built and school gardens to provide fresh vegetables were encouraged with much success. Seeds, expertise and irrigation equipment were provided. This program did not fall directly under me although I was on this national committee. The main drive came from Win Coaker, a remarkable woman.

In 1968 I was appointed Director of the Food Aid Program in Lesotho, a position I held until I left Lesotho on retirement by the end of 1969. At least 100,000 children were being fed lunch five days a week.

Malnourished children. Note the enlarged abdomen due to kwashiorkor — protein deficiency.

Left: Herd boys looking after cattle. Boys like these often started school in their teenage years. The different age groups starting school together often caused problems.   Right: Happy and well nourished schoolchildren.

School children carry water for cooking the lunchtime meal or watering the vegetable garden.

Nearly every village had a school. The three missions (Roman Catholic, Anglican and Paris Evangelical) ran the school system, subsidised by the Lesotho Government. In 1960 the literacy rate was about 70 per cent.

Right: United Nations food donated and used by Save the Children Fund for the school feeding scheme. 100,000 school lunches were provided five days a week through the efforts of Save the Children.

School vegetable garden.

Food and Fodder Relief

By light plane and helicopter in the rugged mountain terrain of Qachas Neck, Lesotho, 1963

In the winter of 1963, as District Commissioner, I was instructed by Head Office to co-ordinate and help with food and fodder relief for an area which had been all but buried under an exceptional fall of snow. The area was remote with small villages scattered along the mountain slopes. A lot of sheep and cattle were grazed in the area and they were starving and so were the villagers. The snow was so thick that people were marooned in their villages and the animals could not graze. The only way to help was by way of food drops. Oxfam agreed to pay for the charter of a small plane and a Bell helicopter, also maize meal, kerosene and lucerne bales. We packed the maize meal into five-kilo plastic bags and put each bag into

Cessna plane and helicopter, which we used for the airdrop. Not much cargo space! Lying in the back of the plane with the door off so that we could "shovel out" the food and fodder was a freezing exercise for me and my assistant.

a separate hessian bag and tied it up strongly. The lucerne bales were cut in half and each half put into a hessian bag. We put kerosene into two-litre tin containers.

After completing the arrangements for the food and fodder drop, the pilot took the rear door and back seats off the plane so that we had open floor space. We did a reconnaissance of the snowbound area and selected a number of long flat spaces where the pilot could come in low but not land. A helper and myself took it in turns lying flat in the rear of the plane and as the pilot came in low over the selected "drop" site we would shovel out as many of the hessian bags as possible, then the pilot would come around again and we would repeat the exercise.

Hungry horse in the snow on top of the world.

These two herd boys in a cave had been cut off from their village. They had a small fire going using brush wood.

With the door open it was freezing! Having dropped the food off we would return to base, hop into the helicopter and return. Using the helicopter the dropped food would then be ferried out to those villages that could not reach "drop" sites. A Bell helicopter at nine thousand feet does not carry much of a load!

It was a laborious operation that took us all day.

From the air one could see how the hungry cattle had made forays into the snow trying to reach higher ground and possibly a few blades of grass—mainly they did not get far. At one village as the helicopter came down, an old villager came out of her hut, waving her arms and shouting "God has arrived!"

This lady was collecting snow in her bucket to melt down for family needs. A remarkable picture.

The Pub with no Beer! A traditional beer vendor operated from this hut but he had long since been drunk dry. The beer is made from sorghum and is not highly potent. I found it unpalatable!

The Diamonds of Letseng la Terae

The lure of diamonds brings out the best and worst in people. A thousand people living in primitive conditions at a height of 10,500 feet in a remote and inhospitable location in the Maluti Mountains created a fascinating study in human behaviour. In the first few years there was no sanitation, no hygienically secure water supply, no shop, no telephone, no medical facilities, no road, no transport service. Everyone shared a common goal—to find diamonds and become rich, but the harsh and primitive living conditions brought with them a challenge for survival. Despite all this, people always seemed to be cheerful. The pervading optimism and high morale was nurtured by the fact that they were working for themselves and instant riches were always a possibility.

While I was District Commissioner Mokhotlong the diamond field was within my territorial area of responsibility. I often went there in an administrative capacity and I played a major part in getting an access road built. There was surprisingly little crime but there were a few occasions when I did deal with court work originating from there—the odd assault and some cases of disputed diamond ownership.

Diamond exploration in Lesotho was conducted throughout the 1950s. Certain rivers and streams gave geological indications of the presence of diamonds and it was a case of identifying the location and establishing the potential viability of the diamond pipe or pipes. Letseng la Terae was eventually pinpointed as the location of a significant diamond pipe but of undetermined wealth. The remoteness, rugged terrain and unproven viability was a strong deterrent to exploitation of Letseng la Terae by a major mining company—to get heavy machinery on site and establish infrastructure would have necessitated the construction of an access road through rugged mountain country at huge cost. So the Government decided the diamonds would best be exploited by Basotho miners on small leases. The Government did nothing to provide amenities other than a small tin hut with two police troopers.

Mid-winter on the diamond fields with temperatures going down to -15C. In the 1960s, on average, three hundred optimistic miners stayed on the fields throughout winter.

The same scene in summer. The huts were built entirely from local materials—stone, mud and thatched roof.

The diamond field was licensed in 1961 by the Lesotho Government for mining by Lesotho citizens only. Leases were small—thirty feet by thirty feet only, and could be obtained through the Government Registrar at a small fee. The marketing of the diamonds found at Letseng la Terae is a story in itself. The De Beers cartel controlled by South African-owned Anglo American Corporation regulated the diamond markets of the world. IDB (illegal diamond buying or selling) was a serious offence in South Africa. Lesotho was in no position to flout the rules of "big brother" South Africa and legislation was brought in to bring diamond marketing in Lesotho into line with South Africa.

In order to provide a legal outlet for the diamonds found on the diggings, diamond buyers from other countries were granted licences.

Fuel was always a problem. These donkeys are carrying a load of sehalahala, a brush wood much used at Letseng la Terae for cooking.

Pack mules in winter. On this occasion we took food funded by Oxfam into Letseng la Terae for the use of miners when they were isolated for some weeks by heavy snow. The iron building is the Police Station. We used four pack mules to carry the food and I had four staff accompany me. In some places the snow was so deep that a mule would find itself unable to reach firm ground and it would flounder, with its body held up by the snow. My staff and I were on horseback; we sent the animals ahead the day before and rode from the road-head 22 miles on a jeep track. On the day we rode the snow was still thick but the sun came out; the glare was blinding. Then we had the 22 miles back on horseback the same day. We were all exhausted by the end.

This miner (and family) had sold his six hundred sheep to buy mining equipment —when I spoke to him he had been mining six months and had found nothing.

This miner invested just about nothing in equipment and in his second week found a big diamond. He used much of the money to fly down to Mokhotlong and back every two weeks to buy alcohol.

Diamond buyers from South Africa and further afield showed strong interest in Letseng la Terae diamonds in the early stages but its inaccessability saw a diminishing number visit the place. The six hundred-yard airstrip at a height of 10,500 feet in a single-engine plane or an eight-hour round trip on horseback was not for the fainthearted or physically ill-equipped.

These are recollections which stand out regarding diamond buyers. An Austrian diamond buyer in his late fifties and overweight, returning from a flight to Letseng la Terae, on alighting from the plane remarked to me, "Mr Nettelton, I am a diamond buyer, not an adventurer." He never returned. On another occasion four diamond buyers found themselves stranded at Letseng la Terae when the weather closed in and they were unable to fly out. There was no such thing as a local hotel where they could spend the night so they hired horses and rode three hours to Tlokoeng from where they were able to get a Land Rover to drive them to Mokhotlong, another one and a half hours. They arrived at our house at ten o'clock at night, in the middle of a lively party involving some other travellers also stranded by the weather. The Mokhotlong Hotel had burnt down so we put them all up overnight. Our Mokhotlong house was elegantly furnished and well stocked with food and drink. Gail was still in her twenties—vivacious, pretty and an excellent hostess. The contrast between Letseng la Terae living and a night at our house was stark. All in all it combined into a great party and our stranded travellers were so very grateful. The diamond buyers got together and sent us a very expensive set of cut glass wine glasses.

It was not long before Basotho leaseholders were being financed by European entrepreneurs from South Africa, most of them pretty shady characters. The Europeans often used their Letseng la Terae partnership as a way to market through legal channels diamonds obtained illegally in South Africa. This worked for them up to a point, but a good diamond buyer can usually tell the exact mine from which a diamond comes so the ploy did not always work.

Some smart African con men in Lesotho learnt fast! One of the tricks was to get pieces of glass, boil them for a couple of days in milk by which time they acquired the look and oily feel of a diamond, then pass them off to the unwary as diamonds. I recall an occasion when a diamond buyer who should have known better bought four pieces of glass doctored in this way and paid a handsome price for them. He only realised his mistake after he had returned home. The con man disappeared and probably bought himself a flock of sheep in a far away part of the country. The diamond buyer never got his money back. On another occasion a South African European who was not a diamond buyer came to see me about the regulations concerning car registration, which I explained to him. He departed. Later I learnt on the grapevine that he had been approached by an African petrol attendant in Maseru with some "diamonds" for sale. A diamond transaction of this nature was of course highly illegal. The European agreed to buy the diamonds. The African suggested the vehicle driven by the European would be a fair price and this was agreed. The

Sunsets were often dramatic with cloud swelling over the Drakensberg escarpment which drops a sheer 3000ft about twenty kilometres away.

African was no fool and required that the two of them go to the Motor Vehicle Registration Office and have the vehicle formally transferred into his name; not before this was done was he prepared to hand over the diamonds. The transfer of the vehicle registration was duly completed and the diamonds changed hands. The European returned to South Africa and subsequently realised he had been conned. The car was legally registered in the African's name and the purchaser was in no position to take legal action because to do so would have resulted in a charge of IDB being brought against him.

I remember an occasion when I was dealing with a court case involving theft of a diamond worth about 10,000 rand (in those days $10,000 Australian). We had house guests and I adjourned court and went home for lunch. The diamond (Exhibit "A") was in a plastic bag on the bench and I agreed with the prosecutor that it would be best if I put the diamond in my pocket for safe custody during the lunch break. At lunch I pulled it out of my pocket and handed it round the dining table still in its plastic bag asking what they thought it was worth. I got answers between a piece of glass and a few hundred dollars!

Letseng la Terae produced some big stones over the years but they weren't gemstones, mostly industrials. The biggest find was a 600-carat stone found by an African miner working with his wife. It was at that time the seventh-biggest diamond ever found in the world and it sold for half a million rand. The miner used his money to buy a trading store with house and peacocks on the lawn near Mafeteng in the lowlands of Lesotho. The new owner had no business experience and went broke a few years later.

Very few miners were able to use their newfound wealth to establish themselves in lasting financial security. They lived for the moment and were overwhelmed by the demands of friends and relatives. Be this as it may, the diamonds of Letseng la Terae brought times of happiness and fulfilment to people who would never otherwise have had the opportunity to experience wealth and the dignity of working for themselves.

Over the years the individual small leases got deeper and deeper and became impossible to work without sophisticated machinery. Eventually the Lesotho Government terminated the small leases and granted a mining lease to the mining conglomerate Lonrho. By then road access made heavy machinery feasible. The mine never proved to be rich and was ultimately closed.

Gail alongside a Cessna used to fly passengers and urgent supplies into Letseng la Terae. The airstrip was six hundred yards long and 10,500 feet above sea level—not for the fainthearted. High winds were often a problem.

In 1963 we got a Land Rover through to the diamond fields. In 1964 a jeep track was built from Tlokoeng to Letseng la Terae, a distance of twenty-two miles, thus establishing a link with the Mokhotlong jeep track network.

There were some wonderful characters working their leases. They were working for themselves and they worked so hard.

Lesteng la Terae 'Busy Bee'. The camaraderie on the diamond fields was notable.

Morale was always high — tomorrow we will find that big diamond! The oldest profession thrived!

Mokhotlong Roads in the 1960s

The 'roads' in the Mokhotlong District in the 1960s were no more than jeep tracks, very often just a bit of an upgrade of the original bridle paths that were made for horses and pack animals. It was in the first years just after the Second World War (1946 onwards) that four-wheel-drive vehicles first made their appearance, brought up the Sani Pass. My first experience of the Sani Pass was in 1957. There were twenty-three reverses on those hazardous bends to get even a short wheel base vehicle to the top!

By 1962 when I became District Commissioner Mokhotlong, the Pass had been greatly improved through the efforts of Bob Phillips, surveyor and road builder. It had become possible to travel the forty-four miles (seventy-three kilometres) from Himeville at the bottom of the Pass to Mokhotlong in three and a half hours. We could also reach villages such as Molumong and Rafolatsane by vehicle. Our trips were subject to the weather, ie snow and rain.

Fair weather and the red hot pokers are out! Travelling in such conditions was most enjoyable.

Bob Phillips (left) and Bill Bright. Bob surveyed many of the mountain roads in Lesotho and played a vital role in the administration of road building projects in the mountains. Bill was director of Mokhotlong

Mountain Transport which operated from Himeville in Natal. They both played a very important role in pioneering a reliable and regular transport service from Natal up the Sani Pass to Mokhotlong and also to Letseng la Terae.

Crossing the Sani River in flood on way to Ann Duncan's wedding in Natal.

Crossing the Orange River. The technique I used was to keep my revs high, slip the clutch and edge my way across.

Clearing snow on the jeep track at Kotisephola (Black Mountain) at a height of 11,000ft (3300m).

Vehicle gets through the "tunnel" cleared by prisoners on Black Mountain. Pascalis, my District Office driver, is on the right—a remarkable man.

Travelling after a snowfall.

Almost stuck.

Gail used a surf board to do some tobogganing.

Jeep travel on Black Mountain in good weather.

The same track after a snow fall.

Mokhotlong Gaol

The hard labour for the prisoners was generally not very taxing but clearing snow drifts in winter was hard work. It was an hour's drive from the gaol to the snow and they travelled in the back of a long wheel base Land Rover, usually leaving at daybreak and getting back to the gaol after dark. It would have been a very cold day but we never had any complaints or trouble. I remember one occasion when one of the warders lined the prisoners up and popped an aspirin into everyone's mouth. He said it prevented frostbite!

Road gang off to work.

When I acted as District Commissioner in Mokhotlong in 1958 the gaol was a dark and dingy place made of local stone. By 1962 when I went back to Mokhotlong a new gaol had been built using Besser block. It was well ventilated and felt hygienic.

Mokhotlong Fun and Recreation

Tennis at Mokhotlong.

During the three years that I was District Commissioner at Mokhotlong, with the labour supplied by the prison population I managed to get two nice tennis courts built, a cricket pitch and a very rough golf course. The tennis courts were used a lot and we had

Local cricket

a regular Saturday afternoon get-together for quite a long time. There were some good players amongst the African population.

One of the enjoyable aspects of the tennis was that there always had to be a referee who conducted a running commentary on whichever match was in progress. It really was quite fun to hear this commentary going on, such as, "And now the DC has put a good service into the left-hand corner and Mr Ramopetla has slammed it into the net. Good service and bad return." And so it went on. I remember one tennis player who was one of the rebels of the district and who caused me endless trouble administratively. During the course of one of these tennis afternoons he told me quietly that if I was interested, his wife would always be available for me! Needless to say I never availed myself of his kind offer. Yes, the tennis was good fun.

The cricket was a little less successful as there were not as many players among the population as there were tennis enthusiasts, and of course one needs a lot more people to get up a game of cricket. However we had a nucleus of enthusiastic players and what I did was to get some of the prisoners up from the prison to do the fielding. I always remember a notorious stock thief who had caused us endless trouble who we placed fielding in the covers and when a fairly hard cover drive hit him on the shin he jumped all over the field, saying that the ball was just too hard. The cricket didn't last all that long but we had some good matches with the help of the prisoners.

Golf seemed to be confined to just half a dozen of us. It was a very rough little course where one played preferred lie and the greens were from a fine gravel sieved by the prisoners. I doubt that any golf or cricket has been played at Mokhotlong since my departure but I hope the tennis courts have survived.

The Christmas Party

Health inspector disguised as Father Christmas!

The Christmas party at Mokhotlong was a great occasion for the children. Gail was the main instigator and she rallied the ladies and harassed the shopkeepers and managed to raise enough money so that each child got some sweets, a small plate of jelly, a tiny present and a balloon and I think a cracker and a couple of other little things.

The health inspector was a tall good-looking man. Gail made a Father Christmas outfit for him from crinkly paper and he really looked the part. In the first year we got about sixty children who came along and in the second year we got one hundred and twenty; in the third year I think we found ourselves with half the child population of the district. Gail was terrific.

Sweets and jelly for children at the Christmas party.

Craft Exhibitions

The schools and a number of ladies' organisations made handcrafts from clay, grass or bead work. The standard was not particularly good but the exhibitions were well patronised by everyone and there was a lot of pride in the work.

Crafts

Races: The one-horse race

The race meeting on the Mokhotlong Airstrip was an annual event. The total number of competing horses never exceeded eight and there were four races of varying distances. Prize money for the Mokhotlong Cup, the main event of the afternoon, was R5 (five rand). On one occasion there was a dispute between race horse owners and the outcome was that only one horse ran in the Cup. The R5 was duly claimed and paid. The sole bookmaker at the carnival declined to take any bets!

Winner of the Mokhotlong Cup — only one horse ran!

Cinema Night

The DC's house in Mokhotlong was wired for 220-volt electricity so we bought a new 3KVA generator, petrol-operated, which we put in the unused stables. We used our electricity in the house for lights only and this gave us some surplus so I arranged for power lines to be taken up to the Courtroom two hundred yards away, and on Friday nights we had a film show which was hugely popular with the African community. I was able to arrange a permanent loan of a projector from the Education Department and the British Council in Maseru sent us films weekly on the plane.

Weddings

There were some elaborate and expensive weddings in Mokhotlong. Some couples were married in church and in other instances I conducted the service. As DC I was a proclaimed marriage celebrant.

A local wedding

Village Garden Competition

In the summer months vegetables grew very well and we held an annual garden competition confined to those who lived in the village. Competition was keen and the judges had to be on their mettle!

Garden competition

Gail and I grew root crops such as carrots, potatoes and onions and stored them for the winter. We sold any surplus vegetables in aid of the Red Cross.

Partridge Shooting

There was good partridge shooting on the mountain slopes with good grass cover. We used to go out on horseback, four of us spread out in a line, and flush the birds out. They never flew more than fifty to a hundred metres. We would note where any settled and dismount and walk up to them. They sat very tight and would get up in a flurry of wings and we used a shot-gun, shooting as they flew. They were not an easy target but we usually came home with a useful bag. Andrew Storm the local trader was an exceptional shot. A nice partridge is good eating.

Engine problems after a partridge shooting outing — normally on a Sunday.

Vocal Groups

The Basotho sing beautifully and they love to sing. This group at right were entertainers and the male vocalist had a truly superb soprano voice. He made the hairs on the back of your neck stand up.

Entertainers

We decided to take the risk and took most of our personal furniture up the Sani Pass by Land Rover over very rough roads — we did not have a single breakage. With Gail's expertise and a bit of wallpaper we were able to set up a very stylish  house way up in the mountains. We had many a good dinner party.

Prize cauliflower

In my official capacity as District Commissioner a great deal of entertaining was required which Gail and I did at home — especially after the hotel burnt down. Gail was a great hostess and we had a lot of fun in our 3½ years at Mokhotlong. Our visitors' book makes interesting reading.

Mokhotlong: Upgrade of the Residency

In 1958, I spent four months at Mokhotlong as acting DC. It was very cold but by then a lot of money had been spent on upgrading government infrastructure in Mokhotlong. A new two-ward hospital with operating theatre and various other facilities was built. The DC's house was wired for 220 volts but not current. An anthracite stove had been installed which was not just to cook on but it also heated the water in the bathroom. So we had steamy hot water twenty-four hours a day. It worked well. An anthracite stove heated the sitting room also. The house was quite cosy and cooking on the big anthracite stove was a great bonus.

In Lesotho we had nine districts, each with a DC who was the senior representative of the British in their own district. Each district had a Residency which was always occupied by the DC. Every residence had

Above: Spring garden at the Residency

Winter at the Residency

a flagpole on which the Union Jack was flown. The flag was raised every morning seven days a week and lowered at sunset. A police trooper was assigned to this duty. The symbolism of the flag was that the sun must never set on the Union Jack. The DC had the privilege of four prisoners and a gaoler assigned solely to his household five days a week. The Residency normally included about five acres of land, much of which was devoted to growing fodder for his private horses which he used on work-related excercises such as treks into the mountains. In Mokhotlong we had a beautiful and colourful garden in summer and a highly productive vegetable garden. The soil was very fertile and an irrigation furrow led from a spring on the hillside and flowed through the garden. The asparagus bed was phenomenally productive. There was the inevitable outdoor cat which was passed from one DC to the next.

Ernest James and Muriel Turner (Gail's parents) in front of the DC's residence at Mokhotlong, right, and in the garden, below.

Daughters Beverley and Tanika in the garden at Mokhotlong.

This man was serving a six-month jail term for stock theft — I had dealt with his case. There was no animosity towards me. A real day's work!

Mokhotlong: Traditional Scenes, early 1960s

I took these photos as I moved around in the early 1960s. Old traditions still were often adhered to, especially in the more remote areas way up in the mountains.

Ladies with umbrellas.

Thatching a hut.

Right and middle: Threshing wheat —no machinery!

Women hoeing— traditional, laborious women's work. The men plough, sow and reap.

Herd boys in cattle country high in the mountains where the sheep and goats were taken often during the winter months. These little boys, it will be noted, had not even been given a proper blanket and depended on an old sheepskin to keep themselves warm.

Donkey transport for firewood.

Elderly lady in remote village. She tried to sell me duck eggs. I don't like duck eggs so there was no sale.

Basotho court — these courts dealt mainly with civil matters and were distributed throughout Lesotho. The Basotho love litigation. The system allowed for an appeal from a Basotho court to the Judicial Commissioner, a qualified jurist.

Traditional musician

Thatching a hut in a remote mountain area. The normal rondavel had seventeen, usually poplar, branches taken from the ravines, and were thatched with wheat straw.

Chief Leabua Jonathan
Prime Minister of Lesotho, 1964-1977

The Prime Minister wearing the traditional Basotho hat.

In the years 1964 to 1969 I knew Chief Leabua well. During that time I worked directly to him as my Minister in the portfolios of Director, Independence Celebrations, Secretary to the Prime Minister and Director of the Food Aid Program.

Chief Leabua was a descendant of King Moshoeshoe the First, the founder of the Lesotho nation. Leabua was a fairly minor chief in his own right but he had a lot of ability and an easy charm. I first got to know him in the 1950s when he was a member of the Leribe District Council. At council meetings he was always very dapper in double-breasted suits and was always constructive and easy to deal with. At that time I was a District Officer and later on a District Commissioner.

Chief Leabua's formal education was limited to Year 7 at school but he was a great reader. He understood the realities of life in that he did not come from a family of any particular wealth and he had to spend time working as a contract labourer away from home in the gold mines in South Africa. There he learned what hard work was and how to mix with his ordinary fellow beings in a situation of economic survival.

In the early 1950s Chief Leabua became involved in the affairs of the country and worked for a number of years as Assessor to the Judicial Commissioner. His participation in politics increased and his ability was recognised. He was a member of a number of delegations which went abroad on various issues, was a member of the Lesotho Constitutional Review Commission and was chosen as one of the three advisers to the Paramount chief.

In 1959 Chief Leabua formed and became the leader of the Basutoland National Party (BNP). In those days there were three main political parties in Lesotho: the Basutoland Congress Party (BCP) which obtained much of its funding from Russia, the Marema-Tlou which obtained most of its funding from China, and the Basutoland National Party (BNP) which got most of its funding from South Africa. Chief Leabua was a member of the delegation which went to London in 1964 to seek responsible government for Lesotho. The Secretary of State agreed to a process whereby elections would be held in 1965 on the basis of total adult suffrage, and that total independence would be granted twelve months later provided circumstances merited it.

When the first elections were held in Lesotho in 1965 the BNP, led by Chief Leabua, was not expected to win but they benefited greatly from the almost universal support of the senior traditional chiefs and a late injection of funds and the gift of four-wheel-drive vehicles given by the South African Government. South Africa was extremely apprehensive that either the BCP or the Marema-Tlou parties might win the election and provide a base in close proximity to South Africa for elements hostile to themselves, and therefore they felt it was in their interests to give every support they could to the BNP.

So Chief Leabua in 1964 found himself rather unexpectedly as Prime Minister of Lesotho. At that time I was District Commissioner at Mokhotlong, and nine months before the date set down for the independence of Lesotho I was transferred to Maseru to take charge of the organisation of independence celebrations. That is a story in itself and I'll devote a separate section to that. In the organisation of the celebrations, which was a full-time job for nine months, I worked directly to the Prime Minister and found him a very understanding and intelligent boss to deal with. The independence celebrations were a great success and immediately afterwards he asked me if I would take on duties as his Secretary. This I was quite happy to do and I spent eighteen months in that position.

Chief Leabua was essentially a conservative in his political think-

The Prime Minister and seven of his Cabinet Ministers, 1966.

ing. He often admitted to me that he preferred dealing with a British Conservative government to Labour. He was not well disposed towards Middle Eastern countries. He distrusted them, but this is probably explained by the fact that he had had little opportunity to get to know them.

One of the biggest problems faced by Chief Leabua in the role of Prime Minister of a newly independent African nation surrounded by South Africa was to walk the tightrope between retaining his respectability in the eyes of the African nations and not antagonising South Africa. The economy of Lesotho was almost totally dependent on South Africa. He played the role with great skill and Lesotho should thank him for that. He was the first African Prime Minister to hold one-on-one talks with a South African Prime Minister on South African soil.

Chief Leabua was a good politician but the continual wrangling and upheavals of the internal politics of the country got him down at times. He loved to travel abroad and don his immaculate suits and make well-delivered speeches, and to enjoy all the trappings of a Prime Minister travelling abroad and the courtesies that were extended to such persons. I travelled with him to Malawi, South Africa, Swaziland, United Kingdom and the United States. We stayed in the best hotels including the Waldorf Astoria in New York, and stayed in Blair House in Washington, the guesthouse of the United States President. I had to admire the aplomb with which Chief Leabua could make a speech to the General Assembly of the United Nations or chat with President Lyndon Johnson or speak with total confidence with a British Cabinet Minister.

I wrote many of his speeches and drafted many letters which he signed and acted as his adviser on many issues but I always refrained completely from becoming embroiled in the domestic politics of the Basuto people or his political party. As a European, to have got involved in those sorts of things would have been unacceptable to the Basuto people.

I often found myself in situations where Chief Leabua and myself would be on a foreign trip and we would dine together as a twosome and we had some fascinating discussions. He always proclaimed his total support for a democratic system of government and said he welcomed the fact that he had a strong opposition in Parliament in Lesotho because it kept him on his toes. I was disappointed that a year after I left, scheduled elections were held and as the counting progressed it became evident that Chief Leabua's party was going to lose the election, and he and his Cabinet had all the opposition candidates arrested and put in jail with the excuse that they were guilty of intimidation and electoral fraud. The leader of the opposition, Ntsu Mokhehle, remained in jail for the next seven years. Most of the other opposition candidates were more fortunate and were released after a year or two. Chief Leabua and his Cabinet had control of the Police and Army and therefore he was in a position to enforce his clampdown.

Fresh elections were not held in Lesotho for another twelve years. Chief Leabua remained Prime Minister until shortly before his death in 1977. Despite Chief Leabua's undemocratic behaviour in the 1970s I like to remember him as I knew him when I lived in Lesotho. In those days he was a really nice person and he conducted the affairs of state with a great deal of decorum. I rather suspect that he was pushed by his Cabinet, in particular the Deputy Prime Minister Chief Maseribane Sekhonyela. I never got on with Maseribane and always felt he was self-seeking and devious.

Chief Leabua had seven children. He was married to Mofumahali Mantahli.

Chief Leabua met Dr Verwoerd, Prime Minister of South Africa, in 1966. Dr Verwoerd, the architect of apartheid, was murdered in the South African parliament later that month. Chief Leabua was the only Prime Minister of an independent African country to meet Dr Verwoerd.

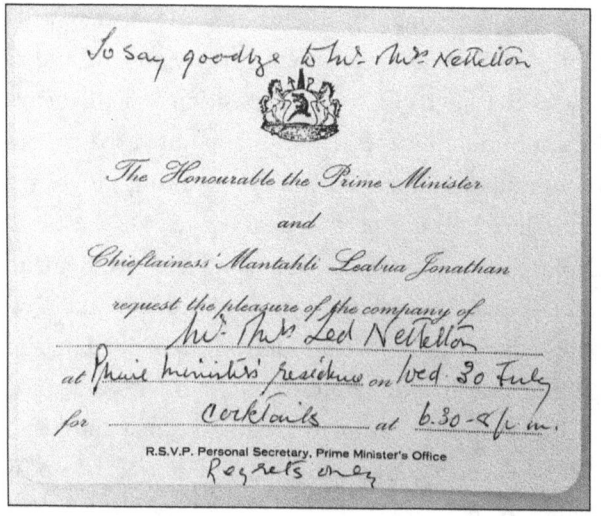

Chief Leabua held a cocktail party to farewell us when we left Lesotho.

Post script

Looking back historically I fully accept that Chief Leabua acted undemocratically in staging the coup of 1990. But I quite honestly believe that Chief Leabua's actions and the subsequent manner in which he managed Lesotho's relations with South Africa and other African nations was masterly and saved Lesotho from a lot of potential strife both economically and politically.

Politics between Lesotho and South Africa in Lead-up to Lesotho Independence and just after (1961-1966)

This period was one of considerable delicacy for both Lesotho and South Africa. The apartheid policies within South Africa were being enforced and extended further and further. A non-white person had to endure the following indignities and many more:

- On trains, third class only for non-whites and not very comfortable.

- In post offices, separate entrances for whites and blacks.

- Public toilet facilities in cities all but non-existent for non-whites.

- Hotels, restaurants, sporting facilities all strictly segregated—those for non-whites very inferior.

- Pass system — non-whites had to carry a pass issued by the government authority of the area in which they lived if they wished to visit or seek work in a different locality.

- No voting rights for parliament, local councils, or other government bodies.

- Non-whites not allowed to be employed in designated jobs.

- Separate beaches for blacks and whites.

- Separate schools.

- Buses segregated.

- Group Areas Act made it illegal for non-whites to acquire property in designated white areas, ie: almost everywhere.

- And a lot more.

I took this picture in 1980 on the beach near George in the Eastern Cape, South Africa. Its apartheid message is self-explanatory. (TN)

These apartheid rules included Asians but when South Africa developed a booming iron ore trade with Japan in the 1960s, visiting Japanese were awarded "honorary white status". If it was not so hurtful to so many it would almost be funny.

Against this background Lesotho, an all African and impoverished country, totally surrounded by a powerful South Africa (both economically and militarily) had to shape a pathway of co-existence. South Africa genuinely wanted to live in harmony with Lesotho but I have no doubt that South Africa would have exacted harsh retribution on Lesotho if its government purposely behaved in a way which was hostile to South African interests or security. I believe it was fortuitous that Chief Leabua became Prime Minister of Lesotho at this critical time.

To exacerbate Chief Leabua's delicate position even further, the non-white governments world wide were expressing their distaste for South Africa because of its apartheid policies and the British Commonwealth of Nations were collectively threatening to expel South Africa from the Commonwealth. Chief Leabua had to delicately conduct the affairs of Lesotho in such a way that he did not upset South Africa on the one hand but retained his respectability in the eyes of his African colleagues on the other. It was a delicate tightrope walk and he managed it brilliantly. He established good diplomatic relations with South Africa and there was an exchange of meetings quite frequently between senior representatives, but Chief Leabua refused to set up an embassy in South Africa and made it clear that should circumstances change he would insist that his Ambassador to South Africa would be a black man.

Chief Leabua reached the stage where Dr Verwoerd, Prime Minister of South Africa at that time, agreed to meet him in his office in Pretoria for face-to-face talks. Things had come a long way! The African nations turned out to be extremely understanding of Lesotho's delicate relationship with South Africa and Chief Leabua experienced no condemnation of his successful co-existence formula with South Africa. Chief Leabua also played a big role in the harmonious transition within Lesotho of the transfer of governmental power from a predominantly white-controlled hierarchy to a new African regime —political control, public service and also social interaction. His easygoing, friendly and non-threatening attitude towards the white section of the community, both government and private sector, was much to his credit.

Against this background the South African press—English, Afrikaans and African, took a keen interest in the Lesotho/South African relationship because it had implications for South Africa's ability to forge good terms with other African countries as well as Lesotho. Malawi, under President Banda, was the only other African country to establish a relationship with South Africa.

Chief Leabua always refused to accept extensive aid from South Africa even though it was there for the taking, but President Banda went for broke and as a result he extracted huge aid packages from South Africa—even built a whole new capital city at Lelongwe in central Malawi which South Africa paid for. In that era South Africa was very wealthy—the South African rand bought $1.20 AUD.

Souvenir program from Lesotho Independence celebrations, 1966. A Nation is born.

Lesotho Independence Celebrations
October, 1966

Lesotho gained independence from Great Britain at midnight on 4th October, 1966. In January of that year I was appointed officer responsible for organising the celebrations. I found myself with a big task which occupied me fully for nine months. I started with a secretary, two clerks, one typewriter and a single office which had no telephone. From these humble beginnings I moved to a position of forty-nine work teams each responsible under my coordination for various segments of the celebrations. Forty-eight countries attended the celebrations represented in various ways from Presidents to ministers to Ambassadors. Princess Marina represented the Queen. She was such a dignified, friendly person. I really liked her.

The funds allocated initially were totally inadequate. The attention of the politicians was concentrated on a constitutional crisis involving the Prime Minister and the king and we all wondered whether Independence would really be achieved in October as planned—but we had no option other than to keep going as if everything was going to be fine. In the end the constitutional crisis sorted itself out and the celebrations took place on time.

The opposition Basutoland Congress Party lead by Ntsu Mokhehle advocated to his followers that they should boycott the celebrations, but two weeks before Independence Day he changed his mind and withdrew the boycott threat and advocated that his followers attend in a peaceful way. I am convinced that Mokhehle knew he would be backing a loser if he persisted with the boycott threat—in the last few weeks before Independence Day there was a fast-developing excitement, even euphoria, building in the community, the exact opposite to a boycott of the celebrations.

A mounted escort was provided for both the King and Princess Marina.

Her Royal Highness, Princess Marina, Duchess of Kent, representing the Queen, delivers the articles of Lesotho Independence to King Moshoeshoe II at a midnight ceremony on October 4th, 1966.

The four most prominent people at the independence celebrations. Left to right: King Moshoeshoe II, King of the newly independent Kingdom of Lesotho; Sir Alexander Giles, Resident Commissioner of Lesotho and therefore the senior resident British official at the time of independence; Her Royal Highness, Princess Marina; and Chief Leabua Jonathan, Prime Minister of Lesotho.

Statue of King Moshoeshoe I, Founder of the Basotho Nation

I found myself landed with the task of commissioning the statue and supplying the sculptor with pictures of King Moshoeshoe I. We sought artistic guidance from various sources in South Africa and finally chose Eugene Leon Bouffa, a well-known Belgian sculptor domiciled in South Africa.

The King's private secretary, Gray Qhobela, and I flew to Pretoria to see Eugene Bouffa. We authorised him to proceed immediately as time was getting short. He did a good job, although I have always felt that the statue looks more like the King's private secretary than King Moshoeshoe I as depicted in historical drawings. The unveiling of the statue as part of the independence celebrations was a memorable event. The statue dominates Maseru from a hill to the west of the town and is floodlit at night.

The statue of King Moshoeshoe I, unveiled in October 1966.

King Moshoeshoe II, mounted and wearing a "royal" red patterned blanket, arrives at an Independence ceremony.

The King's followers all on horseback and in their red blankets and traditional basotho hats.

New Lesotho Flag and Coat of Arms

My office found itself responsible for the design of the new coat of arms. I commissioned Maseru architect Clive Househam. The King, Prime Minister and cabinet liked the design and approved it. We went into full operational mode with production of flags, distribution of the design for souvenir products, circulated to government departments, schools, etc. Three huge royal standards were requisitioned from a South African flag manufacturer. It was all go.

Then the bombshell! Professor Dennis Cowen, who didn't like me and felt that he had not been adequately involved in Independence Celebration issues (he played a leading role in drawing up the new Lesotho constitution) produced a letter from a UK heritage authority stating that the tails on the horses in our new coat of arms design were drooping instead of being rampant. A drooping tail denotes cowardice! There was no alternative but to go into damage control. It was too late to change much of the printed material, souvenirs etc. We did get new flags produced in time including the royal standard. We did not publicise the crisis and the vast majority of people never knew.

Over a period of time, the adjusted coat of arms gradually took over. After a few years it was no longer an issue. I have a set of beer mugs which I treasure with the "wrong" coat of arms on them.

The new Lesotho flag—green, red and blue, with the traditional Basotho hat in white—flies proudly in the breeze at the Independence Ceremony on October 4th, 1966.

Colour version of the first Lesotho flag. This design was retained until 1987, when the flag was changed for the first time. It was altered again in 2006 to the design in place today.

Princess Marina

Princess Marina was accompanied by her personal secretary, Sir Philip Hay, and her lady in waiting. She was a very natural person, no airs or fancies, and not at all demanding. She stayed at the British High Commissioner's residence hosted by Ian and Suzie Gray. The only special arrangement we had to make for her accommodation was to have her bedroom curtains heavily lined so that the morning light did not wake her early.

Right up to the last day the King was still a bit grumpy about the new constitution and his place in it although he had agreed to abide by it. We all had that undertone of nervousness that he might do something unexpected at the Independence Celebrations. As things turned out the King behaved admirably and carried out all his duties as King cheerfully and fully.

I also got on well with Sir Philip Hay. On certain occasions he took time off and left me to accompany Princess Marina on his behalf.

When Tracy was born two weeks after the celebrations, Princess Marina sent a telegram of congratulations. The year after the celebrations Gail and I visited the UK and Princess Marina invited us to Wimbledon — complimentary tickets and tea in the royal tent. Also there were Princess Margaret, Harold Macmillan (ex British Prime Minister) and a host of other dignitaries. It was quite an occasion for us!

Left to right: Sir Philip Hay, Princess Marina, Lady in Waiting, Ted Nettelton.

Some Interesting Recollections of Independence Celebrations

1. A new thatched stadium was built for the celebrations. It was a large, elegant structure supported by wooden poles. Five days before the celebrations were scheduled to start, part of the stadium collapsed. The thatching experts worked twenty-four hours a day to repair the damage and it was finally completed with thirty-six hours to spare. The collapse occurred where all the VIPs were to be seated. The consequences of the collapse happening during the ceremony are too horrific to contemplate.

2. The stadium looked great with a green mat of grass. In fact it was wheat—sown six weeks before by Bob Phillips.

3. The Bloemfontein band engaged for the Independence Ball at the Palace got lost and arrived an hour late. We were at panic stations. Twenty-four hours earlier we were also at panic stations: the builders finished the new Royal activity centre where the ball was to be held with just hours to spare and then the marquee which housed all sorts of things blew down the day before. In the final outcome the ball was a great success. Gail made her ball gown from sitting room curtains—looked great.

4. A pitso (gathering) was held two hours' drive up the mountain road for the purpose of involving people outside Maseru, the capital, in the celebrations. Most of the foreign dignitaries attended. Special toilets were erected. However, someone locked them and no one knew where the key was. The VIPs endured six hours in all without access to toilet facilities. About 3000 people turned up for the mountain pitso.

5. An Ambassador from a Mediterranean country was chauffeured by a member of my staff—a pretty, young blonde woman. They vanished for twelve hours and we were at panic stations again. They resurfaced full of smiles and with an implausible explanation. I called the lass to my office. She confirmed she had in no way been ill-treated so I let the matter drop. I certainly did not want to stir up a diplomatic issue. The press would have loved it!

6. VIP seating was a nightmare. The diplomatic fraternity are notoriously touchy. I allocated seating on the basis of the person's status in their own

country, e.g. a president as against simply an ambassador. We then used an alphabetical formula with Commonwealth taking precedence over non-Commonwealth countries. The Egyptian Ambassador made a great fuss because he felt slighted by the fact that the representative from a small Commonwealth country such as Sierra Leone was placed ahead of Egypt. It took a lot of sorting out.

...Long Hours of Hard Work
— an excerpt from the Lesotho Quarterly

'The weariest man in Maseru at the end of Lesotho's week-long independence celebrations during October was undoubtedly Ted Nettelton, who was mainly responsible for ensuring the success of the festivities.

A cheerful smile from Ted Nettelton, the Independence Celebrations Officer, whose hard work and unflagging enthusiasm ensured the success of the festivities.

'Mr Nettelton, appointed Independence Celebrations Officer at the beginning of the year, built up to an almost 24-hour working day by the time the celebrations got under way — yet throughout he tackled his job with an infectious enthusiasm and good humour that did much to rouse the flagging spirits of his fellow workers.

"It was easily the toughest job I've ever had," he said when it was all over. "The organisation needed and the close attention to details meant that everyone — not only myself — had to put in long hours of hard work. But it was worth it in the end: I think our celebrations were enjoyed by everyone, despite the fact that most visitors had already had seven days of Botswana's festivities first."

Fresh back from Maluti Mountains, where he had spent a few quiet days fishing for trout after the celebrations ended, Mr Nettelton relived the hectic months of preparation in a special interview with Lesotho Quarterly.

"Things started quietly enough in January, when I was appointed," he said. "I opened my office on January 23, in the District Commissioner's building in Maseru, and began by trying to read as much as I could of other independence ceremonies.

"One of the immediate problems, however, was finance. Lesotho is a small country and there were many things more important — on a long-term basis — than the independence celebrations that needed money. Government accordingly voted R50,000 for celebrations, a small sum compared to, say, Botswana, where R150,000 was voted. In fact, the amount was the smallest ever voted for an independence celebration in Africa. Because of this, it was decided to organise an appeal fund for the celebrations."

The Lesotho Independence Celebrations Appeal Fun was launched in February, with conspicuous success. From the start it was decided to approach only business houses, industries and prominent individuals who had had business dealings with Lesotho in the past. A total of about 200 letters was sent out, resulting in a magnificent response.

"We raised about R36,000 in cash, plus about a dozen scholarships for varying amounts tenable at different institutions," Mr Nettelton said. "These latter, while not contributing directly to the celebrations, will be of inestimable value to Lesotho in the years ahead. "Apart from this, the two banks in the territory — Barclays and Standard — each donated R10,000 on the understanding that the money would be used to establish a permanent museum in Maseru."

Mr Nettelton's next job was to obtain a decision on the date of the celebrations, how long they should last and what events should be held.

"The Government decided on October 4 as the Independence Day for a number of reasons," he said. "Firstly, there was sufficient time between the date on which it had been agreed Lesotho could ask for its independence (April 29, 1966); secondly, we knew that the Botswana celebrations would be taking place the week before, and it seemed more convenient to the countries sending delegates to both festivities to follow immediately after; and thirdly, the first Monday in October is always a public holiday and is traditionally a period of festivity."

— Lesotho Quarterly

FIREWORKS WILL CALM EMOTIONS

STAFF REPORTER

FIREWORKS may cascade into the night sky as part of Basutoland's independence celebrations—but strictly for their tranquillising effect.

As the Union Jack is lowered at midnight on October 4 and the flag of the independent Kingdom of Lesotho goes up in its place, Maseru's traditional pitso ground is expected to be jammed with up to 100,000 emotional celebrants.

After a solemn pause of 30 seconds, say some members of the celebrations committee, a fireworks display will be necessary to distract the crowd and relieve tension.

"Fireworks may be regarded as an extravagance for a poor country, but some of us are going to press for them as being vital for crowd control," a Basuto told me.

MAN IN CHARGE

Mr. Ted Nettelton, a 34-year-old former district commissioner, has been made celebrations officer. He is working with a committee of Basutos and Whites to ensure a full programme of events for the proposed four days of countrywide ceremonies.

Under consideration are float processions, traditional dancing and singing, a race meeting and a football match. There will probably be meat and beer handouts for the mountainfolk who visit the towns, and the overflow of visitors is likely to be accommodated in private homes and schools.

As a guide, Mr. Nettelton is studying the form freedom celebrations took in other African states.

He and his men are busy making up the guest list now.

"Just like any hostess we shall have to be very diplomatic about it all," he said. "But there are always those who feel they should have been invited to one or other of the functions. I imagine that the wisest thing for the celebrations officer to do is to slip out of the country before it's all over."

MR. TED NETTELTON
... may slip out.

Glimpse of Tensions on Night of Independence Celebrations

I have included in these memoirs the transcripts of Princess Marina's authority from the Queen to represent her at the Lesotho Independence Celebrations and Her Majesty's message of goodwill wishes for prosperity — it makes for a nice personal anecdote.

On the evening of Independence Celebrations there was still a lingering uncertainty as to whether King Moshoeshe would accept the independence papers which Princess Marina was due to hand to him at a midnight ceremony in front of 30,000 people. The dispute between Chief Leabua's government and King Moshoeshe was still simmering. The King was aggrieved that the new constitution took away from him most of his former political authority and relegated him to an essentially ceremonial role — very much in the Westminster style. I was part of the small group assembled at the British High Commissioner's residence due to accompany Princess Marina to the ceremony at the Maseru showgrounds. I well remember her striding up and down the sitting room as we waited for the chauffeur-driven cars to arrive when she stopped, looked at us and said "If he does not accept these documents I will hit him over the head with them, push them into his hands and tell him to go and get on with things on his own." She then strode on. As it turned out, King Moshoeshe behaved admirably at the ceremony and everything went like clockwork. But post independence the bad blood between Chief Leabua's government and King Moshoeshe festered on until the King was eventually forced into temporary exile.

The flag-raising ceremony had gone ahead without a hitch. Motlotlehi behaved with great dignity. What a relief. Princess Marina, representing the Queen, and King Moshoeshoe II in a friendly chat — all is well!

The following transcripts are from photocopies taken by me of the original papers that Princess Marina read on that night.

Copy of Letter of Authority signed personally by the Queen designating Princess Marina to act on her behalf at the ceremony at which the Kingdom of Lesotho was granted Independence by Great Britain.

HRH PRINCESS MARINA, DUCHESS OF KENT
INDEPENDENCE CEREMONY — LESOTHO
4TH OCTOBER, 1966

"The Queen has entrusted me with a personal message from Her Majesty to the people of Lesotho. It is now my very great pleasure to read you this message:

> 'I have asked my aunt to act as my representative at the celebrations of the independence of Lesotho.
>
> I visited your country in March, 1947 with my parents and my sister. That visit left me with very pleasant and vivid memories. I recall in particular the warmth and kindness with which we were welcomed, the great gathering at the Royal Pitso on Moshesh Day, your horsemen and your mountains. I appreciate the pride which you must feel today as your country returns to independence and my thoughts are with you.
>
> It is with great pleasure that I welcome you to our Commonwealth of Nations. I send you my good wishes and I pray that God may guard and guide you in the years to come'."
>
> SIGNED .... ELIZABETH R

Speech made by HRH Princess Marina at the Independence ceremony on 4 October 1966:

> "Motlotlehi*,
> It is almost a hundred years since Moshoeshoe, the great founder of your nation, brought his country under the protection of her Majesty Queen Victoria. At that time, as you know, the very existence of the Basuto as a powerful and unified people was seriously threatened. Today we can give thanks that these threats were not fulfilled, and that Moshoeshoe, the man with whom so many had found refuge, himself found refuge with that great and good Queen. The Basuto were preserved as a unified nation, and now, after nearly a century, the colony of Basutoland becomes the independent Kingdom of Lesotho. On this proud and happy occasion, I bring to you and to your people the congratulations of Her Majesty The Queen, and to these I would like to add my own.
>
> The way in which your people have attained to their independence has been the way of peaceful and steady advance. There have invariably been stresses and strains, but these have been overcome by mutual goodwill and understanding. I fervently hope that in the years that lie ahead you will continue to advance peacefully and steadily.
>
> 'Peace,' as the great Moshoeshoe said, 'is the Mother of Nations.' And again — 'Peace is like the rain which makes the grass grow, while war is like the wind which dries it up.' No doubt there will continue to be stresses and strains in the next few years, but it is the prayer of all who have the real interests of the Basotho at heart that these too will be overcome by goodwill and understanding, that Lesotho will progress both economically and politically, and that she will come to take an honored and respected place in the international community.
>
> The relationship between Basutoland and Great Britain during the last century has almost invariably been the happy association

---

* Leader, or one worthy of praise

of members of the same family. This friendly relationship, firmly based on mutual respect and trust, has twice withstood the tragedy of world-wide war. The willingness with which so many Basuto came to the help of Great Britain, and the great sacrifices which they made in two world wars, will always be remembered and with lasting gratitude.

Motlotlehi,
It is now my duty — and indeed a great privilege — to hand to you the Constitutional Instruments whereby the Independent Kingdom of Lesotho is established. May this Kingdom flourish and prosper and may it enjoy those three great blessings which it had so wisely chosen as its motto:

Khotso, Pula, Nala*."

---

* Peace, Rain, Prosperity.

Hans Richter-Haaser

About four months before the celebrations I noticed that a piano recital tour of South Africa's four main cities by Hans Richter-Haaser, a noted German classical pianist, coincided with the Lesotho celebrations. I wanted to diversify our program to suit the tastes of as many people as possible, so I thought "Why not give it a shot?" I tracked down the person organising Richter-Haaser's tour and put to him the most unlikely possibility that Richter-Haaser might give a single recital in Maseru; we would fly him from Johannesburg to Maseru where he would give his concert in the evening and we would fly him back the next day. But we could not afford a hefty recital fee.

Program from the performance of Hans Richter-Haaser in Maseru during Independence celebrations.

To my amazement the message came back a week later that he would be honoured to be part of our celebrations and that there would be no fee. All he asked was that we handle his travel and accommodation and that we pay for this part of the exercise. There was no air service in those days between Maseru and Jan Smuts Airport, Johannesburg (since renamed) so I arranged to charter a small plane and I flew up to Johannesburg to escort him back to Maseru. It was a two-hour flight in a single-engine Cessna. We had a good chat in the plane; he was a modest, charming man.

The concert was staged in the Roman Catholic Cathedral, a handsome sandstone building with high vaulted ceilings. The concert was packed with people of all cultures and creeds and was a huge success. The next day we flew him back to Jo'burg. It says a great deal about Richter-Haaser that he agreed to our request. The single-engine Cessna did not faze him as it did many people from European coutries. As mentioned earlier in the volume, I remember one Austrian diamond buyer who had flown to the remote diamond mine located 10,000 feet above sea level with a dicey air strip to boot. As he got off the plane he said, "Mr Nettelton, I am a diamond buyer, not an adventurer." He never came back.

Political Controversies Before and After Lesotho Independence 1966

The clippings on the following pages offer a short look at the realities of apartheid South African government attitude to an all-African state on its borders and the deportment of other neighbouring nations, through the lens of contemporary newspaper coverage.

TIMELINE

Leabua Jonathan relationship with white South African political leaders

Leabua Coup 1970—all newly elected opposition parliamentarians arrested.

Leabua Jonathan, tough politician but basically a gentleman.

Leabua may ask Dr. V. to freedom party

By RALPH COHEN

DR. VERWOERD would be invited to Basutoland's independence celebrations, Chief Leabua Jonathan, Prime Minister of Basutoland, intimated to me in Maseru yesterday.

Asked if he feared that an invitation to Dr. Verwoerd would upset North African states, Chief Leabua replied: "They would be well advised not to oppose Dr. Verwoerd's presence. Their transit through South Africa depends on him. In any event, we shall invite any Head of State whom we want to invite."

Talking of grain and Basutoland's shortage of food, Chief Leabua said he would gladly accept another gift of grain from South Africa.

"But the Basuto people are self-respecting. And in our self-respect we never want to pester generosity by asking for more than we are given."

S.A. HELP

Plans for the country's October independence celebrations are well in hand, according to Government spokesmen — and South Africa may help financially.

A number of South African firms have been asked to help sponsor a big turf club meeting as part of the independence celebrations, and it is hoped that good stakes will attract South African entries.

An accommodation shortage in Maseru may force the Government into the peculiar position of housing guests in South Africa. All hotel accommodation in Maseru has been reserved by the Government — as well as an entire hotel on the South African side of the Caledon River.

An hotel project that was to have given extra accommodation in Maseru has been dropped. "It's all a bit embarrassing," said a Government official.

Chinese representatives have already booked in at the South African hotel.

ISSUE COMING TO A HEAD

Waiting for a simmering Basutoland to boil over

The Friend Africa News Service

MASERU.

BASUTOLAND for several years the watched spot of Southern African politics is simmering perceptibly at last. To most observers the only outstanding question now is not whether it will boil over, but when. The fresh crisis sparked on Tuesday by Prime Minister Leabua Jonathan's call to Paramount Chief Moshoeshoe II to choose between the Paramountcy or party politics, continued to escalate on Wednesday.

It was nudged on its way by the news that the Paramount Chief — in clear defiance of the Premier's ultimatum — will hold a mass rally on Sunday week to put his point of view to the people.

With this announcement came a rumour that the opposition parties now touting abroad Chief Moshoeshoe's claim that he should retain control over the Police, the Army and Foreign Affairs, will urge their supporters to boycott the independence celebrations on October 4.

If true, such a move would tend to counter Chief Jonathan's invitation to the opposition last Sunday to "join hands with the Government" in preparing for the celebrations.

Meanwhile, public reaction to the abdication challenge has been one of shock and dismay.

Even many supporters of the Government feel that Chief Jonathan should have stayed his hand until the Paramount Chief had given some indication that he intended carrying his anti-constitution campaign beyond his promise to report back to the Basuto nation on the independence talks.

They believe the Prime Minister may have harmed his own image by this strong attack on the man who is after all the traditional head of the nation and the Queen's official representative here.

Opponents of the Government are saying that Chief Jonathan should have had the courage to issue the challenge to the Paramount Chief at last Sunday's public pitso — and not in a mere Press handout.

With the best will in the world it is impossible not to feel uneasy about Basutoland. All the ingredients for trouble are there — an open rift between head of state and head of Government, a Pan-Africanist opposition seeking support for its cause outside the country. Still Basutoland's best insurance against disaster however, is the fact that the Government and the Opposition parties are so evenly matched.

While constitutional change remains feasible the territory may yet confound the top watchers.

The Friend, Bloemfontein

Rand Daily Mail 18 March 1966

The World, Wednesday June 29, 1966

Jonathan tells King to quit— flies to London

WORLD REPORTER

CHIEF LEABUA JONATHAN, the Prime Minister of Basutoland, flitted out of Jan Smuts Airport, Joburg, last night, without seeing any Pressmen. He boarded a B.O.A.C. flight at 7.45 p.m. for London, where he is to continue negotiations for financial aid for his country.

The Premier had, however, broadcast a statement over Radio South Africa explaining his reasons for inviting the Lesotho Paramount Chief, Moshoeshoe II, to abdicate. The invitation came yesterday and has caused a world-wide stir.

At Jan Smuts Airport, airport officials and police refused to allow a World reporter to see Chief Jonathan in the transit lounge. A policeman waved away the reporter and the airport manager said that Chief Jonathan was "resting" and did not want to be disturbed.

However, a copy of the late edition of yesterday's World, containing the full story of his sensational invitation to the Paramount Chief, was handed to him by South African Government protocol officials.

MASERU QUIET

Meanwhile in Maseru last night, the World learnt that Jonathan's statement had received the backing of many people.

Maseru, which since last night has attracted many pressmen, was said to be quiet.

DESMOND SIXISHE, the World's special representative in Basutoland, reported today that Chief Jonathan's statement was issued only minutes before he was driven to Bloemfontein's J.M.B. Hertzog Airport to board a connecting flight to Joburg and then London.

In his statement, Chief Jonathan said it was time for him to "clarify, by making a statement on the political activities of the Paramount Chief."

He said: "The political activities of Moshoeshoe II have caused widespread comment in Ba___ ___ and abroad."

PASSED BLUEPRINT

Chief Jonathan pointed out that in spite of all efforts made by the Paramount Chief the National Assembly—which again assembles on Friday—and the Senate, had passed his independence blueprint.

"No attempt was made by Paramount Chief to conceal the fact that rallies he has addressed recently were in fact organised by party political interests in opposition to Motlotlehi's Government. They were aided, I regret to say, by political refugees who abused our hospitality by interfering in our affairs," the Prime Minister said.

Chief Jonathan said he had informed the Paramount Chief formally and in writing that the collective advice of his Ministers was that he should not attend or address any meetings and to do that would constitute a departure from established principle.

NOT DISPUTE

Chief Jonathan said he wanted to make it clear that his Government would in no way dispute the powers already held by Motlotlehi under the present constitution.

The Prime Minister challenged the Paramount Chief, that if he "sincerely feels that it is his duty and in the best interests of the nation to engage in politics," to abdicate and give way to a Regent — "then his differences with the elected Government can be fought out fairly and squarely."

'Troops' report raises a grin

WORLD CORRESPONDENT

MASERU.— Basutoland is grinning at a report published in a South African newspaper saying that British troops may be sent there soon.

The report was published soon after two officers of the Royal Irish Fusiliers from Swaziland had visited the territory on a routine ins___

A Government official said: "There is no truth in the rumour."

Moshesh says, 'I will not abdicate'

MASERU.—The Paramount Chief of Basutoland, Moshoeshoe II, said here last night "I have no intention of abdicating." He was commenting on a statement earlier yesterday by the Prime Minister, Chief Leabua Jonathan, inviting him to abdicate or quit the political arena.

The Paramount Chief said that this was a preliminary statement based on a cursory study of the Prime Minister's announcement and that he was still studying this document.

"I succeeded to the Paramountcy as of right and by the express will of the people while certain individuals were opposing me for their own interest.

"If the Prime Minister has, in fact, said that I should abdicate I wish the people to remember that in the years 1959 to 1960 it was not his intention that I should succeed to the Paramountcy."

AT OXFORD

During that period the Paramount Chief was studying at Oxford University and had been proposed by the College of Chiefs as a successor to the then regent.

The Paramount Chief said that when Chief Jonathan, who was then an advisor to the Paramount Chief, resisted his appointment "the people resisted him."

—SAPA.

SCIENTIST TO LECTURE

DR. G. van Praagh, one of the organisers of the Nuffield Science Teaching Project will visit Swaziland, Basutoland and Bechuanaland in July and August. He will give lectures on the Nuffield approach to science teaching.

LECTURE DATES

Between July 15 and 28 he will lecture to teachers at the University of Roma, Basutoland. From August 3 to 10 he will lecture at a selection of Swaziland secondary schools.

He then goes to Gaberones in Bechuanaland, Zambia and Kenya before returning to Britain at the end of August.

His tour has been arranged by the British Council.

The World, 29 June 1966

Jonathan criticises political interference

The Friend Africa News Service

MASERU.

THE PARAMOUNT CHIEF of Basutoland, Moshoeshoe II, said here last night: "I have no intention of abdicating." He was commenting on a statement earlier yesterday by the Prime Minister, Chief Leabua Jonathan, inviting him to abdicate or quit the political arena.

The Paramount Chief said that this was a preliminary statement based on a cursory study of the Prime Minister's announcement and that he was still studying the document. "I succeeded to the paramountcy as of right and by the express will of the people while certain individuals were opposing me for their own interest.

"If the Prime Minister has, in fact, said that I should abdicate, I wish the people to remember that in the years 1959 to 1960 it was not his intention that I should succeed to the paramountcy."

During that period the Paramount Chief was studying at Oxford University and had been proposed by the college of chiefs as a successor to the then regent.

The Paramount Chief said that when Chief Jonathan, who was then an adviser to the Paramount Chief, resisted his appointment "the people resisted him".

"I many now be employing different tactics and taking advantage of his position as Prime Minister, but I am not frightened. I, therefore, place my fate in the Basuto people whom I love and dedicate myself serving them at all times."

Prime Minister Jonathan, in a strongly worded Press statement yesterday, attacked the Paramount Chief's entry into the recent constitutional dispute in which the tribal head of state sought to retain control over the territory's army and police.

The Paramount Chief, Chief Jonathan said, could not have it both ways. "He cannot continue to engage actively in party politics and at the same time enjoy the status and dignity and legal immunity as the representative of Her Majesty the Queen."

The political activities of the Paramount Chief had caused widespread newspaper comments at home and abroad which suggested that there was confusion and uncertainty among the Basuto people.

A regent

If the Paramount Chief sincerely felt it was his duty or in the best interests of the nation to engage in politics, "the Basuto people will allow him to abdicate from his present position and give way to a regent."

The Premier added: "His present differences with ourselves, his elected government, could best be fought out fairly and squarely in the political arena."

Such an abdication would be "indeed a grave and serious matter", but the present constitution allowed for a regent to take the Paramount Chief's place.

The Paramount Chief, said Chief Jonathan, seemed to be uncertain about his own position and this uncertainty could be cleared by his choosing between being a ruler or a party politician.

The Government in no way disputed Chief Moshoeshoe's special powers under the independence constitution. — his control over Basuto land rights, his power to nominate 11 Senators in the Upper House, and his control over the chiefs.

"But he should be above politics, and he must act upon the advice of the Cabinet in all matters except where the constitution gives him special powers."

Prime Minister Jonathan, who left for London later yesterday evening to attend further pre-independence talks, also warned South African political refugees not to take part in Basutoland politics.

There had been no attempt to conceal the fact that the meetings held by the Paramount Chief before the independence conference were organised by party political interests, "aided, I regret to say, by political refugees who have abused the Basutos' hospitality by interfering in the affairs of Basutoland".

Chief Jonathan said he was also aware of the activities within Basutoland of organisations such as the Pan Africanist Congress of S.A. which had been "busily cooperating with subversive and disloyal elements of the Opposition".

The Government was prepared to do what it could to assist refugees in genuine distress. But no country could allow unrestricted access to criminal fugitives or subversive elements whose profession was to create "political instability".

The Premier concluded: "I wish to make it clear to these people that I am delivering the final warning".

Chief Jonathan flew to London from Bloemfontein's J. B. M. Hertzog Airport yesterday afternoon.

Chief Leabua Jonathan.

Moshoeshoe II.

29 June 1966

The Friend, 29 June 1966

RAND DAILY MAIL, Wednesday, June 29, 1966.

MOSHOESHOE: I am paramount of right

JONATHAN: He cannot have it both ways

By RALPH COHEN

BASUTO KING HITS BACK

In a telephone interview he said: "I succeeded to the paramountcy of right — and above all, at the express will of the people."

PARAMOUNT CHIEF MOSHOESHOE II of Basutoland, invited yesterday by Chief Leabua Jonathan to abdicate if he wanted to meddle in politics, told me last night: "I have no intention of abdicating."

He added: "I am not afraid. I will place my fate in the hands of the Basuto people whom I love and have dedicated myself to serve at all times."

The Paramount Chief, the Queen's representative and hereditary leader of nearly one million Basutos, said he had only heard of the Prime Minister's statement.

Moshoeshoe's statement came after the Prime Minister, Chief Jonathan, attacked the Paramount Chief yesterday for holding pitsos (gatherings) that were organised by political parties with the aid of political refugees. These meetings, said Chief Leabua, challenged the policies of the Paramount Chief's own Government.

"Moshoeshoe cannot have it both ways," said Chief Leabua. "If he sincerely feels that it is his duty to engage in politics, the Basuto will allow him to abdicate from his present exalted position and give way to a regent.

"His present differences with his elected Government could then be fought out fairly and squarely in the political arena."

Full control

The crux of the dispute is the new freedom constitution, which was signed in London two weeks ago. The constitution makes the Paramount Chief constitutional monarch after independence, with the limited powers of the British system.

Moshoeshoe believes he should have been given full control of the army, police, internal security, and external affairs to prevent abuse of these powers by the Government.

Chief Leabua would not budge on this issue, in which the Paramount Chief was supported by the powerful Basutoland Opposition Congress Party and the Marematlou Freedom Party.

The Paramount Chief refused to sign the London independence document, claiming it was worthless because it did not have the full support of the people.

Don't meddle

Prime Minister Leabua made a brief but triumphant return to Basutoland on Sunday to assure the people that independence would definitely be granted on October 4.

Julius Malie, the "Rand Daily Mail's" Maseru correspondent, reports that the Prime Minister yesterday gave political refugees in the territory a final warning not to meddle in local politics.

INDEPENDENCE MEANS A TWO-WAY TREK

By RALPH COHEN

BRITAIN will beat a final retreat from Mafeking next month — and South Africa will bow out of Bechuanaland.

In a quick, modern two-way trek, years of historical association will end.

Mafeking will be relieved of its last British civil servants — one of the biggest events since the siege in 1899. And South Africa, after more than 80 years, will stop operating the Bechuanaland section of the Vryburg-Bulawayo railway line.

While 70 families of Bechuanaland civil servants move from the Imperial reserve in Mafeking to the new capital of Gaberones, 40 South African railwaymen and their families will be returning to the Republic.

BRITISH FLAG

The final move to Gaberones, about the middle of the month, will mean that the Bechuanaland civil service will no longer have two "homes". It was only in February last year that the first 150 administrative civil servants moved to Gaberones, ending 70 years of a strange situation in which the protectorate was administered by the British from South Africa.

Now — just three months before independence — homes and offices are ready for all in Gaberones, and the British flag will come down in Mafeking.

Rhodesia will probably be the new occupant of British buildings in the reserve. Rhodesia Railways have taken over from South Africa the Bechuanaland section of the Bulawayo line ... — Ramothlabena

to Mahalapye, and have begun to accommodate their staff in Mafeking.

Rand Daily Mail
29 June 1966

Crisis a big challenge to S. Africa

From Our Political Correspondent

CAPE TOWN. — Lesotho's dramatic constitutional crisis has posed the most serious challenge yet to the South African Government's still controversial "outwards movement."

The whole future of the policy may be wrapped up in the way South Africa responds overtly and covertly to Chief Leabua Jonathan's decision to declare a state of emergency, suspend the Constitution, and arrest the leaders of the Opposition Congress Party.

One of the major objectives of the "outwards movement" is to prove to a sceptical world that "racialistic" South Africa is capable of living in peace with her Black neighbours; that she is capable of tolerating their non-racial policies; that she respects their sovereignty, and that she is capable of aiding them towards prosperity without robbing them of their independence.

Here Chief Leabua Jonathan's conservative pro-South African Government has been defeated at the polls (so far unofficially) by the more militant, more Socialistic and definitely anti-South African Congress Party which is widely believed to have strong links with Communist China.

The problems of co-existing with a Lesotho regime under Congress leader Ntsu Mokhehle would be tremendous.

By the same token, the temptation to covertly aid Chief Leabua Jonathan and thus perpetuate a regime that offers no problems in the realm of co-existence must be great.

However, if South Africa does yield to temptation and if she is caught at it, what credibility she has achieved in the world with the "outwards movement" would be destroyed.

King Moshoeshoe being sworn in as the Queen's representative in Basutoland—shortly before the country became the independent state of Lesotho. "He has abdictated," said Chief Jonathan today.

RAND DAILY MAIL, Thursday, June 30, 1966.

Whip Moshoeshoe into line, British urged

STAFF REPORTER

THE Basutoland Government wants its future king, Paramount Chief Moshoeshoe II, brought to heel by Britain for his involvement in politics.

"We expect Britain to order Moshoeshoe to toe the line," a Government official in Maseru told me. "After all, he is the Queen's representative."

The Prime Minister, Chief Leabua Jonathan, has thrown the ball to Britain by publicly announcing it is her duty, as guardian, to stop the Paramount Chief from being "unconstitutional and addressing political meetings." Political observers believe Britain will have to enter the war of words that has flared up between the Prime Minister and the Paramount Chief.

Tempers can only get hotter as matters are, with the Prime Minister back in London and the Paramount Chief determined to go on with a plan to address pitsos (gatherings) in his absence.

SHOWDOWN

Moshoeshoe says the people are unhappy because Chief Leabua would not give post-independence executive powers to the hereditary leadership. And he wants a mandate "from the people" as to what he should do next.

One sees the Paramount Chief paying scant attention to any admonishing finger from Britain. He is committed to getting control of the army, police, internal security and foreign affairs — just as hard-headedly as Chief Leabua is committed to seeing he does not achieve this aim.

Nerves are taut in Basutoland as the Government and the paramountcy squabble.

The Paramount Chief has made it clear that he will remain monarch and not be tempted by Chief Leabua's offer that he should abdicate and enter politics.

Some think that he has behind him the kernel of a solid party already — the Opposition Basutoland Congress Party and the Marematlou Freedom Party which are backing him to the hilt.

Rand Daily Mail, 30 June 1966

Basutoland to be Lesotho

The Star's Africa News Service

OCTOBER 4, the day of Basutoland's independence, will set the seal on a personal triumph for the 52-year-old Prime Minister, Chief Leabua Jonathan, which began 18 months ago when his National Party was elected to power against all odds.

Since that event the burly former gold-miner has fought stiff opposition from both inside and outside Parliament to entrench himself as the first Prime Minister of the new Kingdom of Lesotho.

He has been more successful than even his most avid supporters could have predicted.

In the Senate he has won over the majority of the 22 principal and ward chiefs, who at one stage threatened to become the Opposition's most effective instrument against him.

He has confronted Paramount Chief Moshoeshoe II on equal terms over the constitutional dispute and in the process has managed to preserve his image of "strength in moderation."

Abroad he has persuaded the British against their instincts to grant him certain powers now—control over finance, the army, the police and internal security—which were due to come his way only after independence.

UNEASE FELT

Now, to crown these achievements, Chief Jonathan has gained for Basutoland the vaunted laurel of independence—and entirely on his own terms.

The Basuto electorate has obviously taken cognizance of the events of the past year and a half. The Prime Minister's personal image has never been brighter.

But at the same time it is impossible not to feel uneasy about the future of Chief Jonathan and Basutoland.

The present situation has all the ingredients for trouble—a powerful pan-Africanist opposition champing at the bit, a monarch discontented by his own civil impotence. And Britain on the way out.

Paramount Chief Moshoeshoe's attitude after independence will be a vital factor.

VIOLENCE

If he decides to go further with his campaign for greater power, he will certainly have the continued backing of the opposition parties, the Basutoland Congress Party and the Marematlou Freedom Party.

With no Colonial Government to restrain these forces, Lesotho could well find itself in the throes of the violence which so many observers have predicted for so long.

Happily, however, Chief Moshoeshoe gives the impression of being too responsible a man to cast his nation into civil warfare.

TRIBES RALLY

The history of Basutoland as a nation stretches back to 1818 when a minor chief of the Bakoena tribe, named Moshoeshoe, gathered together the remnants of various tribes which had fallen foul of the mighty Zulu and Matabele.

The eventual decision to grant independence to the government

CHIEF LEABUA JONATHAN, photographed in Pretoria on his recent historic visit to the late Dr. Verwoerd, becomes a Prime Minister whose powers are the object of criticism by the Paramount Chief, soon to be his king in the British constitutional tradition.

The Star 1966

Moshoeshoe defends new constitution

The Star's Africa News Service

Maseru, Tuesday. 4th Oct.

THE NEW KING OF LESOTHO, Paramount Chief Moshoeshoe II, this morning swore to uphold and defend the constitution of his country, which he opposed in the bitter power struggle before independence.

In a speech after the oath-taking ceremony, the Paramount Chief told his people: "Let us join hands in our national struggle. Together we must build up a great nation. After independence we will have to ensure that the rule of law is maintained."

A colourful crowd, almost as large as the one which saw the British flag come down for the last time last night, packed the National Pitso ground to hear the oath-taking and to see Princess Marina hand over the instrument of freedom to the Paramount Chief.

QUEEN'S MESSAGE

The Basutos were in gay holiday mood and yelled delightedly when an old man broke the police barrier to do an impromptu dance in front of Chief Moshoeshoe and the Prime Minister, Chief Leabua Jonathan.

The two leaders again presented an amiable front and chatted across the vacant principal chair as they awaited the arrival of the Princess.

Princess Marina presented a message from the Queen, recalling a similar gathering at the same ground 19 years ago when she, her parents and Princess Margaret visited Basutoland.

Locals who were present at both occasions said today that last night's crowd was even larger than the royal visit gathering.

In her own address, Princess Marina said she hoped Lesotho would continue to advance peacefully and successfully.

The South African Minister of Foreign Affairs, Dr. Hilgard Muller, was present at the second such ceremony in five days.

However, he will not address the National Assembly as scheduled for Thursday. Government sources here say he will only spend a few hours in the new State today, as he did in Botswana last Friday.

Pressure of work is believed to be the reason for the change of plans. Dr. Muller flies out later this week to attend the current United Nations session.

Dr. Muller was to have presented South Africa's gift to Lesotho—a Speaker's throne for the Assembly—to the Prime Minister. The presentation will now be made by the Deputy-Chairman of Committees of the South African House of Assembly, Mr. J. J. Visse.

The Star 4 October 1966

A PERSONAL TRIUMPH FOR CHIEF JONATHAN

TODAY, THE DAY of Basutoland's independence, will set the seal on a personal triumph for 52-year-old Prime Minister Leabua Jonathan which began 18 months ago when his National Party was elected to power against all odds.

Since that event, the burly ex-goldminer has fought stiff opposition from both inside and outside Parliament to entrench himself as the first Prime Minister of the new Kingdom of Lesotho.

He has been more successful than even his most avid supporters could have predicted.

In the Senate, he has won over the majority of the 22 principal and ward chiefs, who at one stage threatened to become the Opposition's most effective instrument against him. He has confronted Paramount Chief Moshoeshoe II on equal terms over the constitutional dispute and, in the process, has managed to preserve his image of "strength in moderation."

Abroad, he persuaded Britain against her instincts to grant him certain powers nine months ago — control over finance, the army the police and internal security — which were only due to come his way after independence.

Now, to crown these achievements, Chief Jonathan has gained for Basutoland the vaunted laurel of independence — and entirely on his own terms.

The Basutoland electorate has obviously taken great cognisance of the events of the past year and a half. The Prime Minister's personal image has never been brighter.

MODERATION

Prime Minister Leabua Jonathan is a moderate man. Politically, he believes that moderation — particularly in regard to relations with South Africa — is the only code that will give Basutoland a chance on its own in Africa.

For this reason, his greatest danger is Pan-Africanism. Pan-Africanist elements are prominent in the Basuto Opposition. Pan-Africanism has tried to sabotage his image in the rest of Africa by alleging that he is no more than a "puppet of the South African Government".

Yet, ironically, it was a staunch Pan-Africanist—Patrick Duncan—who persuaded Chief Jonathan to enter politics. That was in 1951, when Duncan was Judicial Commissioner in Basutoland and the chief was his assessor.

Chief Jonathan responded eagerly. Even at that early stage, he had a firm grounding in matters of government, and rightly foresaw a time when men with such experience would be needed in the territory.

That same experience — coupled with an astute grasp of complex situations — still comprises his best stock-in-trade, for he can match few younger opponents in the matter of formal education.

Born in 1914, the son of a Leribe chief, Leabua Jonathan attended a mission school until standard six. Then, like so many other young Basuto before and since, he went to work on the Rand mines.

In 1937, he was recalled by Chief Jonathan Matheaira of Tsikoane to assist in the administration of the chief's district. He stayed there until his appointment as Assessor to the Judicial Commissioner.

FIRST SUCCESS

The Prime Minister's first success in politics came in 1956, when he was elected to the Leribe District Council, and shortly after to the advisory National Council.

During the next two years, he travelled to Britain with several delegations. The most important was the 1958 constitutional delegation which led to the Representative Government Constitution of 1960. Chief Jonathan was a member of the drafting committee.

In 1959, he formed the Basutoland National Party—in opposition to the formidable Basutoland Congress Party. During the same year, he attended a course of parliamentary procedure at Westminster.

In 1964—the year before self-government — Chief Jonathan made another trip with a delegation to London. This time they secured the promise from Britain of general elections in Basutoland the following April and—

Chief Jonathan talks with the late Dr H. F. Verwoerd at their historic meeting in Pretoria on September 2.

provided all remained peaceful —independence a year afterwards.

During these discussions, Chief Leabua Jonathan advocated adult suffrage, whereas the Opposition held the view that only taxpayers should vote.

The ability of Chief Leabua Jonathan to organise was shown by the remarkable manner in which the Basutoland National Party grew from strength to strength until it won the general elections in April 1965.

Chief Jonathan was not sworn in as Prime Minister until July 5 when he took the oath of office before Motlotlehi Moshoeshoe II in Maseru. He had then won a by-election at Mpharane after losing his own contest during the general elections.

In September, 1965, the last of the by-elections was held and the state of parties in the National Assembly was:

Basutoland National Party . 31
Basutoland Congress Party . 25
Marematlou Freedom Party . 4

Prime Minister Jonathan travelled to England in September, accompanied by the Minister of Justice, Chief Peete Peete, and Professor Denis Cowen, to effect some adjustments to the constitution which would make the Government machinery run smoothly.

President Nkrumah of Ghana invited him to attend the African Summit Conference in Accra in October. The Prime Minister was not able to attend but chose a personal envoy to attend it on his behalf — Mr A. S. Mohale.

MORE POWERS

In December, 1965, Chief Leabua Jonathan secured more powers from Britain for his Government, and the portfolio of External Affairs, Internal Security and Defence were assigned to his Ministers. Since then he has also established the two departments of Cultural Affairs and Social Welfare.

His main aim is independence and economic viability for Basutoland, the improvement of agriculture, the establishment of secondary industries and the implementation of the Oxbow hydro-electric scheme.

In June the Prime Minister flew to London for final independence talks with the British Government. This followed approval by both the National Assembly and the Senate of his motion for independence — a blueprint for free Lesotho. He was able to fly back to Maseru with full British backing for independence on October 4.

On September 2 Jonathan met the late Dr Verwoerd in Pretoria — thus becoming the first Black African leader to be received by a South African Prime Minister.

4 October 1966

ABOVE: Chief Leabua Jonathan, Prime Minister of Lesotho, in front of his new official R60,000 residence in Maseru. With him are his wife and two youngest children, Mamos, 8, and Thikhai, 15.

1966

Leabua's official residence in the capital. He had a country residence near Leribe, where he was born.

The three Malawi Cabinet Ministers who are due to hold talks with members of the Lesotho Government today passed through Bloemfontein yesterday on their way to Maseru. The visiting Malawians posed for photographers at the J. B. M. Hertzog Airport yesterday. From left are: Mr Ted Nettleton (Prime Minister Jonathan's principal secretary and Chief of Protocol), Mr J. T. Kumbweza (the Malawian Minister of Trade and Industry), Mr G. W. Kumtumanji (Minister of Natural Resources), Mr Aleke Banda (Minister of Development and Planning) and Mr J. J. Becker (deputy chief of the South African Department of Foreign Affairs' Africa Division).

Malawi Ministers visit Maseru

By a Staff Reporter

THE three Malawi Cabinet Ministers, who wind up their 10-day goodwill tour of Southern Africa with a meeting of members of the Lesotho Government today, passed through Bloemfontein yesterday on their way to Maseru.

The Malawians — Mr G. W. Kumtumanji, Minister of Natural Resources; Mr Aleke Banda, Minister of Development and Planning; and Mr J. T. Kumbweza, Minister of Trade and Industry — arrived at Bloemfontein's J. B. M. Hertzog Airport aboard South African Airways' scheduled midday flight from Johannesburg.

They were met at the airport by Lesotho Prime Minister, Chief Jonathan's principal secretary and Chief of Protocol, Mr Ted Nettleton, and Capt. J. L. Baartman of the South African security police.

The three visiting Cabinet Ministers, who were accompanied by the deputy chief of the African division of the Department of Foreign Affairs, Mr J. J. Becker, where shown to the V.I.P. lounge where they posed for press photographers but refused any form of an interview.

Shortly afterwards the party left for Maseru where they were officially welcomed to Lesotho at the Caledon Bridge border post by a deputation led by Deputy Prime Minister, Chief Maseribane, the Minister of Local Government, Chief Matete Majara, and Minister of Agriculture, Chief Sebourne Letsie.

After their arrival in Maseru the three visitors had an audience with King Moshoeshoe and were later entertained to a cocktail party.

This morning they will meet Prime Minister Leabua Jonathan for talks and will follow this meeting with discussions with other Lesotho Cabinet Ministers and senior Government officials.

Later in the day the three Malawi guests will visit the University of Lesotho, Botswana and Swaziland and will attend a debate in the National Assembly.

1967

Basic agreement by Vorster and Leabua

CAPE TOWN.—The Prime Minister, Mr Vorster, and the Prime Minister of Lesotho, Chief Leabua Jonathan, agreed on basic issues and on the fact that differences in political philosophy were no bar to co-operation, according to a communique issued yesterday after their two-hour talks.

Chief Jonathan put certain specific proposals for economic aid and technical assistance to the South African Government and Mr Vorster agreed to have these examined by his colleagues as soon as possible.

They agreed that the Republic and Lesotho should remain constantly vigilant against the dangers of international communism.

Both firmly believed in peaceful co-existence on the basis of equality, mutual respect and non-interference in one another's domestic affairs.

COMMON INTEREST

Their examination of the problems affecting the economic development of Lesotho revealed the close interdependence of the two countries and the need for continued close cooperation to promote still further the common interest, the communique said.

The communique concluded with an appeal to men of good will throughout the world to join Mr and the prime ministers in the pursuit of peaceful co-existence between countries regardless of differences in race or national policies.

Chief Leabua, who, with members of his cabinet, arrived at Ysterplaat air station yesterday morning in a S.A.A.F. Skymaster, flew back to Maseru on the same plane after having lunched with Mr. Vorster and the Minister of Foreign Affairs, Dr Muller, at the Mount Nelson Hotel.

On their arrival this morning the party, who were welcomed at Ysterplaat on behalf of the Government by the head of the Africa Division of the Department of Foreign Affairs, Mr A. H. Barrie, were taken to the Mount Nelson hotel, accompanied by Mr Vorster's Parliamentary private office for the talks.

The talks lasted two hours.

Following Nspe text of the communique:

"The object of our meeting was to put on record and to establish firmer contact, by neighbours ...

CHANGES

... have been significant changes since our first visit to the Basutos over four days later... to Pretoria on October 2nd, 1966. Use the IX reviewed visit to the IX ... on recent ways we lamented in both our countries and in other territories in Southern Africa and beyond. And on October 4, 1966, Lesotho achieved sovereign independence, an occasion when the government and peoples of South Africa rejoiced with the government and people of Lesotho.

"We met in a spirit of good will, and our discussion which was both friendly and frank, ranged over a wide field of bilateral problems and international affairs of common concern.

COMMUNISM

"In examination issues we found ourselves in complete accord, more specifically on the fact that differences in political philosophy are no bar to fruitful co-operation. We both firmly believe in peaceful co-existence on the basis of equality, mutual respect and non-interference in one another's domestic affairs.

"We agreed that our two countries should remain constantly vigilant against the dangers of international communism.

"Our examination of the problems affecting economic development of Lesotho revealed the close interdependence of our two countries and the need for continued close cooperation to promote still further our common wealth.

Heavy rain over Vaal
Staff Reporter

WIDESPREAD rain was reported in the Vaal Dam catchment area last night and hopes were high for a further rise in the level of the dam.

At Standerton, the Vaal was expected to rise after heavy rain all afternoon. Harrismith had 30 inches up to 6 p.m. and more rain was expected. At Vrede it rained "hard" from early evening.

PROPOSALS

The Prime Minister of Lesotho put certain specific proposals for economic aid and technical assistance to the Prime Minister of South Africa and agreed to have these examined by his colleagues as soon as possible.

"Deeply conscious of the ardent desire of our respective peoples that friendly relations between our countries should be strengthened still further, we call upon men of goodwill throughout the world to join us in the pursuit of peaceful co-existence between countries, regardless of differences in race or national policies."—SAPA.

January 1967

'LANDMARK OF CO-OPERATION'
Meeting for the good of Africa, says Jonathan

CAPE TOWN.

THE Lesotho Prime Minister, Chief Leabua Jonathan, said at the private luncheon in the Mount Nelson Hotel yesterday that his meeting earlier in the day with the Prime Minister of the Republic, Mr Vorster, was a "landmark of international co-operation".

Replying to Mr Vorster's toast to Lesotho and its Prime Minister, Chief Jonathan said: "Your excellency and gentlemen, on behalf of my Government and my Ministers and officials and advisers here today, I would like to express my unqualified satisfaction and pleasure in our historic meeting.

"I thank you, Mr Prime Minister, and all your colleagues for your hospitality and your friendliness and generous understanding of my country's problems.

"Everyone knows that I have come to ask South Africa to help my economically embarrassed country.

"We in Lesotho are thankful for the freedom which we have already won. We realise that any help which may now be given will be meaningful only to the extent that it enables the establishment of a stable and prosperous African continent.

'A NEW WORLD'

"We hope for a new world in which each sovereign country will respect the other's aspirations and ways of life. The emphasis should be on encouraging what is potentially good, in a spirit of charitable co-operation, rather than carping on shortcomings. We must be positive and confident, rather than negative and fearful.

"In this spirit, Your Excellency, I sincerely believe that men of goodwill everywhere will soon realise that our meeting in Cape Town today has been a truly historic one, not only for the healthy future of our own two countries, but for the future of Africa as a whole.

"It is indeed a landmark of international co-operation."—Sapa.

January 1967

Abuse heaped on Jonathan and Banda

Dar es Salaam, Thursday.

TANZANIAN NEWSPAPERS yesterday condemned Malawi and Lesotho for considering an economic community with South Africa. The Government party newspaper, the "Nationalist," and the independent "Standard" said Malawi's President Banda and Lesotho's Chief Jonathan were taking a tragically short-sighted view.

The "Nationalist" said: "President Banda was trying to confuse the rest of Africa about the nature of South Africans, by saying it was childish to talk of fighting them."

By the same token it should have been childish to talk—as once "extremist" Dr. Banda had—of ousting Britain from Malawi.

COURAGE

"The fact is that what it wants is conviction and courage to face up to a problem. This would not need repeating if there was not a danger that Dr. Banda's defeatist advice may pass for realism."

The "Standard" said that those who dismissed as a foible Black Africa's bitter hatred of apartheid and colonialism and her determination to end them, risked a rude awakening.

"We believe that while there is widespread appreciation of the economic difficulties facing Chief Jonathan and Dr. Banda, are they so very different from those facing Zambia's President, Dr. Kaunda?"

It would be a mistake for them to hitch the future of their peoples too firmly to the Vorster star, the newspaper said.

RADIO ATTACK

Guinea and Congo-Brazzaville also attacked the two leaders yesterday.

Guinea Radio declared that Chief Jonathan and Dr. Banda formed "the first nucleus of African traitors advocating entente, co-existence and co-operation with racialist South Africa and colonialist Portugal."

A Brazzaville broadcast called them lapdogs of imperialism, meeting to form a new conspiracy against progressive Africa.

In a joint statement issued in Blantyre before Chief Jonathan left for home yesterday, he and Dr. Banda said that force was no answer to the South West Africa problem, or to the problems of Southern Africa as a whole.

It was in the interests of African nations that trade, commerce, technical co-operation and cultural contacts be freed from political ties.—Sapa-Reuter.

1967

JONATHAN DEFENDS LESOTHO'S POLICY TOWARDS S. AFRICA

NEW YORK.

CHIEF LEABUA JONATHAN, Prime Minister of Lesotho, yesterday defended his country's policies of maintaining links with South Africa as the only hope of bringing about change in the Republic.

At the same time, Chief Jonathan reproved those African states which demanded that his nation, which is surrounded by South Africa, adopt a hostile attitude towards the White-ruled Republic.

He told the General Assembly that Lesotho's relationship with South Africa was a matter of geographical, historical and economic necessity, and for that reason it deserved understanding and sympathy.

Lesotho, as a member of the U.N., rejected force as the solution to international disagreements. "On grounds of principle alone, therefore, we cannot contemplate adopting a belligerent and hostile attitude towards South Africa," Chief Jonathan said.

UNTHINKABLE

"In practice, the disparity in resources, and our geographical position makes such a course unthinkable. If we were so ill-advised as to pursue that course, then we, the African peoples of Southern Africa, would be the first to suffer the consequences — consequences that would not befall those who, from a safe distance and either in ignorance of or without reflection on the facts of our situation, urge us to adopt impossible policies."

The one million people of Lesotho yielded to no-one in their rejection of apartheid, Chief Jonathan said, but they lived in one of the poorest countries in the world, surrounded by a rich one.

The only feasible way of combating apartheid, he said, was by gradual and peaceful methods. South Africa's immediate neighbours, in particular, should prove that, as African states, they were capable of running their own affairs competently.

ultimate responsibility for bringing it down lay with Britain, he said.

"But terrorism we deplore and condemn without reservation," he declared.

He believed that Lesotho had come in for "unjustified and ill-informed criticism" on the question of refugees from South Africa.

The Government would never return political refugees to South Africa, Chief Jonathan assured delegates. He and Dr Muller, the South African Foreign Minister, had agreed that safe passage would be granted through the Republic for 25 refugees who wished to leave Lesotho for other countries.

South Africa was also prepared to consider other applications. But, the Prime Minister said, only 25 had so far asked to leave, while another 100 preferred to remain in Lesotho.

GHANA'S CALL

Mr J. W. K. Harlley, vice-chairman of the National Liberation Council of Ghana, in contrast called for the use of force against Rhodesia and for "positive action" against South Africa.

Rhodesia had flouted U.N. resolutions and there was no sense in living under the delusion that sanctions were working. "Ghana is convinced that the use of force is the next, indeed, the only logical step left in this long and protracted effort to save the people of Zimbabwe from the cruel oppression of the minority White settlers," Mr Harlley, who is also Commissioner for External Affairs, said.

The Government of Ghana, he said, was disappointed with the attitude of the big powers towards full-scale economic sanctions against South Africa. If they believed these would be ineffective, then let them suggest alternative measures.

Appealing for big power co-operation on the U.N. decision to take over South West Africa from the Government in Pretoria, Mr Harlley said: "On apartheid and on South West Africa, this is not the time for more dialogues with South Africa. It is the time for positive action." — Sapa-R.

The Friend, Bloemfontein
26 September 1967

AFRICAN REACTION

Sympathy goes to Jonathan

New York, Tuesday.

AFRICAN DELEGATES yesterday reacted with sympathy and understanding to the policy statement of Lesotho's Prime Minister, Chief Leabua Jonathan, on South Africa although they did not agree with his views.

In a cautious statement before the United Nations General Assembly, the Prime Minister offered his country as a link between South Africa and the outside world. He also said the only way to fight apartheid was "by peaceful means."

A delegate of Senegal said: "We respect his views. He spoke on his Government's policy. Their position is understandable. We can say the same about Cuba which is surrounded by hostile countries."

An Ethiopian delegate echoed: "They are in a very awkward position and they have no alternative."

Another African delegate, from Nigeria, said: "He has spoken realistically. The ordinary man whom the Prime Minister represents would not understand what we are talking about here at the United Nations. But if he can't sell and eat, then he would ask what is wrong."

A delegate from the Ivory Coast had the same impression with some reservation. "His expression of the Government is understandable because of the geographical situation. But as an African, and a member of the Organization of African Unity, he should have shared the views of Africans at least in principle.

"The country should have a contact with all other African countries to explain its situation," he said.

Mr. Corneliu Manescu, the President of the General Assembly of the United Nations and U Thant, the Secretary-General were not present when Dr. Hilgard Muller, the South African Foreign Minister, addressed the Assembly.

U Thant left the chamber to attend a special luncheon given in his honour by the Danish Prime Minister, Mr. Jens Otto Krag. There was, therefore, no question of any deliberate walkout by U Thant when Dr. Muller spoke.

Chief Jonathan had also left earlier but the rest of the Lesotho delegation remained seated. — Sapa-Reuter-Associated Press.

The Star, Johannesburg
26 September 1967

Wilson is backing Reds, says angry Leabua

By J. H. P. SERFONTEIN

MASERU, Saturday.

IN A HARD-HITTING, exclusive interview today, Chief Leabua Jonathan, Prime Minister of Lesotho, accused "the Wilson Government" of bedevilling racial and inter-state relations in Southern Africa, of interfering in internal affairs and of supporting the communist-backed opposition parties.

Of the British decision temporarily to freeze financial aid to Lesotho, he said: "I, my Government and my people are fully prepared to go it alone."

The Wilson Government were recklessly prepared to endanger the welfare of one-million people in their attempts to use Lesotho as a pawn to restrict South Africa's influence in Southern Africa, he said.

This was blatant interference. "If Mr. Wilson thinks he will, in this way, force me to surrender my country to the communist-backed opposition parties, which he would like to see in power, he is making a serious mistake.

There could be no doubt now that there had been a "B.C.P. plot to rig the elections."

He went on: "In Southern Africa we need moderate Governments of all races to ensure racial peace and harmony."

Mr. Wilson was acting against the interests of both Black and White.

One-party

Why, for instance, had Britain not summarily suspended aid to Zambia, Tanzania, Kenya and Uganda, Ghana and Nigeria, "which either have unconstitutional government or are in fact one-party states?"

His Cabinet were discussing drastic measures "to counter this stab in the back.

"I have already instructed officials to cut my own salary by half. There will be similar reductions in Cabinet salaries; the whole salary structure of the civil service will eventually be reduced."

The suspension of aid would not affect Lesotho citizens alone; three other groups would also be affected, British officials now receiving pensions; the University of Lesotho, Botswana and Swaziland and the whole civil service.

"When British aid stops on April 1, these groups will be the first casualties."

I understand that the Lesotho Government are considering approaching several West European countries for financial aid. Apparently the financial situation is not as hopeless as is generally believed.

The total Lesotho budget amounts to some R11-million at present. British aid for the next three years would have been only slightly more than R2-million for the first year, tapering off rapidly.

Lesotho's financial position has been strengthened recently by the new customs agreement between South Africa and the three former protectorates.

Mr. Wynand van Graan, director of the Lesotho Development Corporation, told me: "Recent political developments do not affect our future planning at all. There are at present five major development schemes, totalling almost R2-million, under way, and a number of smaller ones.

The clash between the Jonathan and Wilson governments has a long history. It started in 1965, with the British Government planning to hand over to a B.C.P. government and appointing B.C.P. sympathisers in top jobs.

One of the main reasons for Chief Jonathan's recent failure to detect in advance the "B.C.P. plot" has been the attitude of his British-officered Special Branch, many of whose officers have been inexplicably reluctant to track down communist-trained leaders on the run in Lesotho.

1970

Jonathan—clever and very tough

The Star's Africa News Service

MASERU.—Chief Leabua Jonathan rules alone in Lesotho today. He is the law because of his upset yesterday of what would have been one of the only democratic changes of government in a Black African state.

The little herd boy born in Leribe has come a long way. The son of a chief, he had little formal education.

He was low in political rating right up to some months before his National Party, which he formed in 1959, just edged out the opposition parties with a margin of two seats in the 1965 elections.

He lost his own fight in the Manka constituency and this was as much through lack of personal stature as anything else. The chief was knowledgable on the machinery of government—he attended a course on Parliamentary procedure and practice in London—less able at practical politics.

But premiership soon altered that. He is now a shrewd and practical man dedicated to leading the Basotho from poverty to prosperity. He has withstood bitter criticism of being a "stooge" of Pretoria, of turning land-locked Lesotho into another Transkei.

A Visit to the United States
with Chief Leabua Jonathan, Prime Minister of Lesotho, in 1967

In 1967 I accompanied Chief Leabua, then Prime Minister of Lesotho, and his party on a three-week visit to the United States. Chief Leabua met President Johnson and numerous members of his senior staff, made an inaugural speech to the United Nations and went across to Santa Barbara on the west coast near Los Angeles to help establish a peace corp training group, made up of US volunteers, to work in Lesotho.

As Secretary to the Prime Minister I was responsible for all the arrangements for his trip, working closely with the Lesotho Ambassador to the United States, Albert Mohale, who was based in Washington.

It was an exciting trip during which I was lucky enough to meet many prominent persons, including President Johnson in the Oval Office at the White House. It was a trip upon which many names that I had so often read about in the newspapers became real people who I met.

On a trip such as this there are always the highlights. I guess the main highlight would have to be meeting President Johnson and staying with the Prime Minister and his party in Blair House, the official guest residence of the President where all the visiting kings, queens, presidents and so on stay. I slept in a four-poster bed and it was

---

Jonathan to meet Johnson

WASHINGTON.

PRIME MINISTER Leabua Jonathan of Lesotho, will make a one-day visit to Washington tomorrow. He will be greeted by President Johnson and will stay in the Blair House, the official guest house of foreign dignitaries.

The State Department announced that Chief Jonathan was not here on a state visit, but was stopping over during a trip to New York where he would address the U.N. General Assembly.

The Prime Minister will be guest at a luncheon given by the Under Secretary of State, Mr Nicholas Katzenbach, and will meet several Government and business officials. He returns to New York on Saturday.

On September 26-28, Chief Jonathan will visit a Peace Corps training camp near San Diego, California, where 80 volunteers are preparing to go to Lesotho.
— Sapa-A.P.

President Johnson greets Chief Leabua on the lawns of the White House.

quite interesting to speculate on who had slept there before me. The Prime Minister slept in the room in which the Queen had not so long before slept. I well remember arriving at the White House in a helicopter which landed in an open lawned area and we were met by a flotilla of black Cadillacs; these drove our party up to the White House between a guard of honour which is permanently on duty at the White House and is made up of representatives of prominent military units in the United States who serve on a rotational basis. President Johnson was waiting in front of the White House to greet the Prime Minister and the two of them went off on their own for about twenty minutes, during which time our party of five sat in the Cabinet Room. I remember I sat in Robert McNamara's seat. Each seat had a name tag on it and at that time McNamara was Secretary of State for Defence. We were then ushered into the Oval Office and President Johnson had a good long chat, remarkably relaxed, and it was all really very friendly and enjoyable. I remember President Johnson giving the Prime Minister a good lecture on the necessity to ensure that he kept his grassroots political structure strong.

At the United Nations the Prime Minister delivered his speech in a very confident manner. We all thought that it was a good speech, well

The White House

Blair House, Washington

When JFK became President in 1962 it was decided that the whole Kennedy family would be accommodated in Blair House to allow the West WIng of the White House to be fully renovated. The last such renovation had been 150 years before. Jackie Kennedy had a great reputation for good taste and had directed major renovations in other historic buildings in the USA. Jackie agreed to take on the task which took eighteen months, during which time the Kennedy family stayed in Blair House. My room had a single bed with awning and legs like tree trunks. There was other furniture such as dressing table, chest of drawers and wardrobe — all very obviously antique.

A very good dinner was served at a twelve-seater table. We were left to our own devices; no other guests, which suited all of us after an exhausting day.

The Waldorf Astoria Hotel where we stayed in New York.

The United Nations building where the Prime Minister delivered his inaugural speech to the General Assembly.

delivered, but we were disappointed that it did not even get a mention in the next day's issue of *The New York Time*s. It made one realise that Lesotho was very small fry on the world stage. However, back in South Africa in those days of political tension between South Africa and the black-controlled countries of the continent, his speech received wide coverage.

Whilst in New York we stayed at the Waldorf Astoria, which was quite an experience in itself. We were on about the forty-eighth floor and occupied two suites, one occupied by the Prime Minister and his Private Secretary and one Cabinet Minister and then the rest of us occupied the second suite. I thought the decor of both suites was pretty disappointing, being very much a hangover from the 1930s and in need of quite a lot of help. One of the recollections of staying at the Waldorf was one evening on which everyone apart from the Prime Minister and myself went out, and so I had dinner on my own with the Prime Minister. He was very partial to fish, in particular sole. That evening we had sole and we talked a lot. I can remember him saying to me, "Ted, I am glad that I have such a strong Opposition Party in Lesotho because it keeps me on my toes. I really do believe in a democratic system where there is a governing party and an Opposition and it's good if the Opposition is strong." I thought this was pretty encouraging because at that stage he was only a couple of years into his term of office and the Opposition did give him quite a hard time. The next election was due in 1970. After I had left Lesotho the elections were duly held in 1970 and as the votes were counted it became obvious that the Government was going to lose office. The reaction was for the Government to have all the Opposition candidates arrested, many of them in a position where they were just starting to celebrate their election victories. The grounds for these arrests were that there had been intimidation and violence perpetrated by the Opposition and that the Opposition candidates were mainly responsible. The Leader of the Opposition, Ntsu Mokhehle, stayed in jail for about eight years. The others were released at varying times. Chief Leabua's party remained in office for a further fifteen years after this time but their rule was in no way democratic because Parliament remained suspended throughout this time.

While in the United States I always endeavoured to have briefing notes for the Prime Minister available to him on the night before. I tried to cover every movement he would make, the personalities that he would meet, the type of speech he would have to make, very often with the speech notes available to him. I was really proud of him throughout that trip because he conducted himself with a great deal of charm and confidence.

On one occasion I can recall, he was unexpectedly called upon to make a speech to an ex-servicemen's group. There were no notes and no prepared speech. He stood up and spoke extremely well, saying how important ex-servicemen throughout the world had been in protecting democracy and that many of his own Lesotho countrymen had served in the armed forces during the war and that just as he admired his own countrymen, he also admired the ex-servicemen of the United States. This came right off the top of his head and he got such an ovation.

The Prime Minister's visit to the United States got a lot of media coverage in South Africa and in the United Kingdom. The reason for this was that Lesotho is a small country, totally surrounded by South Africa. At that time South Africa's apartheid system was really cranking up a gear or two. South Africa was economically and militarily extremely strong. This was the era in which colonialism was coming to an end and many African countries were gaining their independence, flexing their muscle and saying what they really thought. Apartheid was a huge indignity toward the dark-skinned people of the world and so South Africa in their eyes was the polecat of Africa. No country, other than Malawi, retained diplomatic relations with South Africa. Lesotho was in a very difficult position in that its economy was totally tied up with that of South Africa and so, if it was to survive economically, it had to play ball to a certain extent with the pariah.

Chief Leabua played his cards very effectively by keeping good relations with South Africa but at the same time making it clear that he did not and never would approve of apartheid. The fact that he retained these economic and diplomatic ties was always going to be a matter of potential friction with other African countries but on the whole they were understanding of his delicate situation and did not put him into isolation. The South African Government worked very hard trying to entice him into an appearance of acceptance of the South African Government and its apartheid laws. He accepted quite a bit of aid from South Africa but he never allowed himself to fall into the trap of condoning apartheid.

After the New York/Washington visit the PM and party went to Santa Barbara in California to visit the Peace Corps volunteers who were in training before going to Lesotho.

> ## Leabua starts Peace Corps programme
>
> WASHINGTON, Monday. — The Prime Minister of Lesotho, Chief Leabua Jonathan, will inaugurate the California training programme for Peace Corps volunteers going to his country.
>
> He will visit San Diego from September 26 to 28 to open the training programme of 80 Peace Corps volunteers, the first to go to Lesotho.
>
> The volunteers will teach in secondary schools and work in public health and community development projects in the country's mountain villages.
>
> Chief Leabua is coming to the United States to address the United Nations General Assembly. He will meet President Johnson on September 22. —Sapa-Associated Press.
>
> *Johannesburg Star*
> 18 September 1967

Letter written by Ted to Gail, 1967, from the Waldorf-Astoria, New York.

The Towers

THE
WALDORF-ASTORIA
NEW YORK 10022

My darling Gail,

Life has been very hectic and there has not been much time for play. To ensure that everything runs smoothly – and certainly has done just that so far – means a lot of work. I took the night off yesterday and tried to get into the metropolitan Opera to see Romeo and Juliet, but it was only the second night of the season so stood little chance. I went to see Mary Martin in "I do, I do" at the 46th State Theatre. It was very good but it was such an effort to stay awake that I gave up and went home to bed! That's how hectic it has been! Yesterday most of the party went out into the country but I am afraid I had to ensure that all the briefs for the Washington jaunt were brought up to date and it was just as well I stayed behind because it took me all day. Tomorrow we go to Washington and I will also meet President Johnson.

I have met all sorts of people like Eban, The Israeli Foreign Minister, Caradem, and so on. Presidents of banks like Chase Manhattan are small fry. I am very sorry I missed meeting U Thant this evening but it couldn't helped. New York prices are fantastic and our five days at the Waldorf Astoria already runs to over a thousand dollars! I bought myself a smart leather brief case with combination lock today – on Madison Avenue. Cost me $29 which wasn't bad value at all. The old PM is doing very well and we are not overworking him too badly. At the Chase Manhattan lunch today he sat there puffing his Churchillian cigar as we sat in Rockefeller's dining room on the 60th floor overlooking the East River for all the world as if the building belonged to him. Rockhill was telling us that the excavation of the 90ft deep foundations alone cost 11 million dollars. I told him we could have given him a site for nothing in Maseru. He thought it very funny!

I still wake up in the early hours of the morning. I am skipping Nairobi at my own suggestion because I think it would be an embarrassment to have me there. PM sees Kenyatta on the 1st October. I will spend an extra day in London and meet up with them on the same flight when it reaches Nairobi. We have to come back through New York after the San Diego trip because PM sees Dean Rush in New York on the 29th. We fly through the night to London and PM carries on to Nairobi that night and I continue the next day. That's all. Love to the girls and your parents.

All my love, Ted.

Letter from Ted to Gail, 1967, from Blair House, the President's Guest House.

BLAIR HOUSE
THE PRESIDENT'S GUEST HOUSE
1651 PENNSYLVANIA AVENUE

22nd September 1967

My darling Gail,

It's been quite a day! We left the hotel in New York at 9am and drove to the naval Air Base outside the city where a viscount jet was waiting for our party. It was all done in a very grand fashion with two waiters on board to cater for a party of 10 of us in all. Anything you wanted was there. The flight took about an hour. At the Maryland Air Base, Washington, a very plush helicopter was waiting for our party and we stepped from the aircraft into the 'copter. We were taken on a fascinating "Cook's" tour of Washington from the 'copter and then landed at Presidents Park where the cars were waiting. It is three minutes drive to the White House through the most beautiful parkland. The drive way up to the State House was lined with a guard of honour consisting of a representative from each of the regiments in the States. It was impressive and very colourful. The President was standing below the White House steps and shook all of our hands. He was very nice and cheerful. The PM and President then disappeared on their own and we sat in the Cabinet room. I sat in the Defence Secretary, Mr MacNamara's chair. Each chair has its name on it — great big plush black leather chairs padded right up the back. After about fifteen minutes we all joined the President in his office. This lasted ten minutes or so and after various discussions we all departed for Blair House. This is a truly magnificent residence. It is French Colonial in style and nearly every stick of furniture has a history. Although everything is old the whole building has tremendous warmth. My bed is a four poster with a gold awning! One literally sinks into the carpets. Kings and Queens, Prime Ministers and Presidents all stay here — including Queen Elizabeth when she visited the States.

We had lunch at the State Department — Mr Katzenbach was the host. Once again there is great opulence and every stick of furniture is an antique. It was truly magnificent. The afternoon has been taken up by all sorts of engagements including a press conference at which the PM did very well.

I must end.

All my love, Ted.

Costings

I had charge of the administration of this trip and I think it is interesting historically to note some of the costs. Every cent spent on the Prime Minister's trip was accounted for, down to expenditure on newspapers.

The contingent consisted of the Prime Minister, four of his ministers and a staff of three (myself, Mosito Molapo the scribe, and another man, Mr Rasekoai. During this trip he went in the capacity of Secretary working with me but normally he was an officer in the Department of Foreign Affairs. We all got on well and after I left Lesotho I kept in touch with Mosito. After we had moved to Australia, I remember one occasion when he had been attending a meeting of Commonwealth countries in Singapore and was returning to Lesotho via Perth and he asked me to meet him in Perth for a chat. That would have been a four-and-a half-hour flight for me from our home in Adelaide.

In Washington our eight-member contingent was accommodated free of charge in the President's guest house, Blair House, for one night. In New York we stayed in four two-bedroom suites at the Waldorf Astoria for ten days. The Prime Minister shared with Mosito Molapo, I shared with Rasekoai. I don't suppose it's usual for a PM's entourage or staff to share bedrooms these days but back in the 1960s it was considered essential to keep down costs. Our ten nights did not break the bank. We paid the following:

Per night

10 nights at R105 for four suites = R1050

10 days at R21 per person per day for meals R840

So the total accommodation costs were R1850. This is about $A175 today but of course the rand was strong in those days so this isn't a comparison that provides any value.

The original notes for the trip—all handwritten (and pictured on the following pages)—record that "the air fares present no problem mainly because the United Nations will pay for five delegates (one first class and four economy class)."

To Permanent Secretary for Finance

(PHOTO COPY ON A4 PAPER)

Copy:
PS/PM
PS External Affairs

Expenses of Prime Minister's trip to the United States.

(as Annexures 'A' and 'B')

I enclose a very rough assessment of the expenses of the Prime Minister's trip to the United States. I cannot guarantee the accuracy of these documents but I feel that they can safely be taken as a rough guide to the costs of the trip.

2. The air fares present no problem mainly because the United Nations will pay the air fares of for five delegates (one first class and four economy class). I anticipate that the five whose fares will be paid by the United Nations will be:—

Prime Minister
Min of Agriculture
Senator Letete }
Mrs Hlalele   } will serve on committees until 20/12/67 in New York at United Nations.
Min of Education

The only two fares still to be paid will be those of Nettelton and Rasekoai which will come out of Head 6 B 1.

Head 6 B 1.

3. It will be noted from Annexure 'B' that an amount of R4000 is going to be needed to cover the Prime Minister and party for subsistence and other incidental expenses. Nettelton will be taking an imprest for this amount with him and at the end of the trip will have to produce documentary evidence of expenses. The imprest will be drawn...

※ (What is balance in 6 B 1)

...Head no 7. Section 4 should they be required.

4. A big celebration is being given in New York by the Lesotho Ambassador at the Permanent Mission of the Kingdom of Lesotho to the United Nations. The Ambassador estimates 3000 dollars for this function. This figure is in accordance with New York standards. The celebration will not only be in honour of the Prime Ministers visit to the United Nations but will also combine the Lesotho National day celebration for both Washington and New York. One thousand dollars of the cost will come from the Ambassadors representation allowance and 700 dollars from Head no 7 Section one Sub Head C 5 and Section Two Sub Head H 5. I have told the Lesotho Ambassador to make all efforts to keep expenditure to 2400 dollars. In this way costs are covered, unless there is some hitch in so far as the Ambassador is concerned.

5. A dinner for congressmen in Washington is likely to cost 1000 dollars. I have not yet worked out how this will be paid for and I anticipate having to delay until I have spoken to the Lesotho Ambassador about savings in his estimates. This is the only item for which provision still has to be verified.

Annexure 'A'

Air fares of Prime Minister's Party

		Cost
(a)	Air Charter Maseru/Bloemfontein — Paid from Head 6 Sub Head B Item 1. This covers the whole party.	R 200
(b)	Air fares Johannesburg/London/New York/London/Jburg	
	Prime Minister	nil
	Minister of Agriculture (difference between 1st class and economy class)	
	(Paid by United Nations)	
	2 Secretaries	
	(Paid from Head 6 Sub Head B Item 1)	
(c)	Air fare New York/San Diego/New York	
	Prime Minister	nil
	Min of Agric	nil
	One other	nil
	(Paid by Peace Corps)	
	Air fare of one other	R 212
(d)	Air fare Johannesburg/Maseru on Lesotho National Airways	
	Prime Minister and three others	R 68
	(Paid from Head 6 Sub Head B Item 1)	

Annexure 'B'

A
14/9/67
Rome
Hotel
P.M. Room for the day   R 14
Minister   "   R 10
2 Secretaries   "   R 7
                              31
Meals for all   20   R 50

Prime Minister arrives in morning and departs on same evening.

B
14/9/67 to 17/9/67 (in morning)
London
Hotel
Nights of 14th, 15th & 16th
P.M. accom @ R25 per night R75
Minister " @ R20 " 60
2 Secretaries " @ R15 " 90
Meals
    For the four (Est. of R15 per day ea.) R 240
Incidentals
    taxis, laundry, drinks, etc.
    For the four @ R5 per diem ea.   60   525

C
17th to 26th Sept
New York & Washington
Waldorf-Astoria Hotel
Ten nights @ R 105 for the four   R 1050
Ten days @ R 21 per person per day   R 840
    for meals
Incidentals to be recorded
    as expended   R 500   2390

D
27th & 28th Sept.
Two nights - accommodation provided
for three plus transport.
Incidentals plus expenses of one   R 200   200

                                    Total   R 3165

A Visit to Malawi

by Chief Leabua Jonathan, Prime Minster of Lesotho, at the invitation of President Banda

In 1967 Chief Leabua was invited by President Hastings Kamuzu Banda on an official visit to Malawi. It turned out to be a most successful visit. I went along as Chief Leabua's secretary. Two Cabinet Ministers and a Private Secretary also accompanied him.

A bit of background: At the time South Africa was despised by most African countries because of its apartheid policies and these countries refused to have anything to do with things South African. No African country had diplomatic representation in South Africa. Because economically Lesotho was almost totally dependent on South Africa it was not easy for Lesotho to shun South Africa. Basotho migrant labourers worked in South African mines and sent considerable money back home to their families. Lesotho was a member of the South African Custom Union, once again a source of important revenue for Lesotho. Chief Leabua had to walk a difficult tightrope between not offending too greatly the apartheid regime of South Africa and at the same time retaining respectability in the eyes of the rest of the world, particularly African countries.

President Banda had worked for twenty years as a medical doctor in the UK and was at home with European society and understood its ways. Five years before our visit he had returned to Malawi, entered politics and won the Presidency. On the other hand President Banda didn't give a damn what other African countries thought; he realised there was a financial bonanza to be had by being friendly with South Africa and he established a diplomatic mission in Pretoria. South Africa, despised by most of the world because of apartheid, was delighted to have Malawi as a friend—it helped its image enormously—and it pumped money into Malawi. President Banda obtained most of the money to finance his new capital at Lilongwe from South Africa.

Chief Leabua and President Banda had common ground as regards their relationship with South Africa so the invitation to visit Malawi was logical in getting together two African countries with similar disposition towards South Africa. My observation was that Jonathan and Banda had very different personalities and in everyday circumstances would not have had much in common, but the South African issue brought them together. After his visit to Malawi, Chief Leabua did not maintain a regular dialogue with President Banda.

Chief Leabua was keen to ensure that his trip went smoothly to the extent that he sent me on my own to Malawi two weeks before he was due to go in order to discuss with Malawi officials arrangements for the trip. I flew from Johannesburg via Harare to Blantyre in Malawi. This was a couple of years after Ian Smith, then Prime Minister of Rhodesia, had declared unilateral independence from Britain and the United Nations had imposed trade bans on Rhodesia as a result. Rhodesia, like South Africa, was looking for friends amongst African countries and they must have seen Lesotho as a possible candidate. The Rhodesian authorities got to hear about my trip to Malawi and I was met at Harare airport by a member of their diplomatic service. After an initial chat, and as I had a couple of hours to spare before flying on to Malawi, I was invited to meet more senior officials in the city. I ended up talking to the Secretary to the Cabinet and was asked to convey many messages to Chief Leabua. In brief the Rhodesian Government was offering generous aid to Lesotho and the establishment of a two-way relationship. When I passed the messages on to Chief Leabua he wouldn't have a bar of it and told me to simply ignore them.

However, when Chief Leabua set off on his official visit, we were faced with the embarrassing situation of having to spend some hours in Harare in transit by air to Malawi and the Rhodesian authorities knew when Chief Leabua would be passing through. To the great credit of the Rhodesian Government they laid on a very nice lunch for Chief Leabua and party at the airport and sent a third secretary from their diplomatic service to welcome our party and to ensure everything went smoothly for the lunch. By adopting this low-key response no one was embarrassed and Chief Leabua appreciated their tact, but was still not prepared to enter into dialogue.

President Banda laid on all the trappings for the visit as the invitations

Malawi really laid out the red carpet for Chief Leabua as illustrated by just three of the event programs (above). There was a function a day in honour of the Prime Minister whose visit coincided with Malawi National Day.

 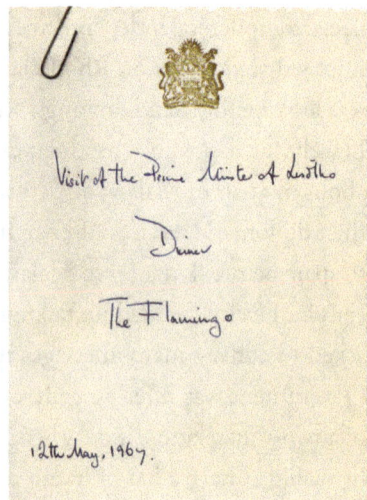

Functions and more functions...

pictured show. In addition to all the official functions there was a half-day flight over Lake Malawi and over the far northern parts of the country.

When Banda returned to Malawi after an absence of twenty years he insisted on speaking only English when addressing meetings so he always used an interpreter. He spoke very fast and I felt sorry for his interpreter. Part of his image was his flywhisk made from the tail of some animal, probably wildebeest. He was respected but feared by all around him. In his early and better years he did a great deal for the Malawian people by

Chief Leabua (on the left) is presented with a leopard skin by President Banda.

Chief Leabua makes an address at the State banquet.

Prime Minister's party taken in Malawi. (I am on the extreme left).

organising projects which worked towards self sufficiency at village level. In those days Malawi became well fed and prosperous. He certainly knew how to manipulate South Africa into providing very substantial aid.

It ultimately all went wrong. One of his early edicts was to get rid of as many Indians as he possibly could because he considered they had taken over commerce in Malawi to the exclusion of the indigenous people. It caused quite a worldwide furore but in typical style Banda ignored the fuss and went right ahead. Banda legislated to make himself President for life but he eventually went totally senile and he was deposed. Thirty years later, like so many African countries, Malawi has huge food shortages and also AIDS problems.

The trip was a great success. The only embarrassing incident was when Chief Leabua's private secretary forgot to bring the gift for President Banda to the farewell function. To his credit President Banda laughed it off.

Chief Leabua's Coup, 1970

"What is your opinion of Jonathan's use of the Police Mobile Unit (PMU)?" — Question to author

Jonathan staged his coup in January 1970 and by that stage I'd been out of Lesotho for about eight months so I was not directly on the scene. I have no doubt at all in my mind that Jonathan felt strong enough to arrest all the Opposition politicians when he knew that he had lost the election, and he must have taken into account the fact that there could have been a big backlash with violence staged by mainly the BCP.

Jonathan would have known that he had the complete loyalty of the police mobile unit commanded by Freddy Roach, and they were indeed a formidable and highly trained group of men. I believe those likely to have caused trouble would have feared them and thought twice before attempting to interfere. On reflection, I believe that Chief Leabua's coup was constitutionally reprehensible and it went against all the values which he expressed to me over quite a number of years. In reflecting back, many years later, I could not help finding myself harbouring a rather contentious view that in the longer term Jonathan's coup was actually in the best interests of Lesotho.

If Ntsu Mokhehle had become PM of Lesotho at that stage the reaction of South Africa to a very openly and fairly militant anti-white PM of Lesotho could have led to all sorts of consequences. Also, the 1960s were a time when both Russia and China were pouring money into Africa. The BCP was being supported by Russian funds and the Marema-Tlou was being supported by Chinese funds. There was great animosity among many Africans towards South Africa and this was quite understandable. I have no doubt at all that Lesotho potentially would have been used as a staging post by subversive African units from South Africa, and not opposed by msheshli (opposition), and these sabotage groups would then have flitted across the border back into Lesotho, an independent country, where South African authorities would not have had the right to make arrests. This potentially would not have gone down well amongst the more extreme elements of the South African government and might well have led to the complete closing down of all movement between South Africa and Lesotho, and the consequences would have been dire.

The fact that Leabua Jonathan behaved in a very unconstitutional manner, and in a way that was very unfair to certain people, nevertheless achieved continued harmony between South Africa and Lesotho which was very much in the interests of the general Basotholand population. I know that in saying that I'm being very controversial, but if you analyse what I've said I think there's a lot of logic in my thinking.

It was reported in one South African newspaper that South Africa had sent a message to Lesotho calling on it to honour the legitimate outcome of the election. I treat this with scepticism. Inevitably South Africa was going to be under suspicion and I would suspect that spreading this type of rumour when in reality they had not sent a message at all would help ease the suspicion directed towards them.

Another factor, which is true amongst elected parliamentarians throughout the world, is that they do not like losing the "goodies" that come with holding office. In my observation this would have been a very relevant factor in Lesotho and it is not only the parliamentarians who benefit; it often extends to family and relatives.

And last, but not least, this coup would not have occurred if Chief Leabua had been without the Commissioner of Police, Freddy Roach, and his 350-strong highly trained paramilitary force standing in the background to deal with any trouble. Chief Leabua knew he could depend on their loyalty one hundred per cent if there was physical violence by outraged Congress Party supporters — there was none!

Chief Leabua died in 1977. He remained Prime Minister until not long before his death.

The Natal Mercury reports on the coup, 31 January 1970

Crisis a big challenge to S. Africa

From Our Political Correspondent

CAPE TOWN. — Lesotho's dramatic constitutional crisis has posed the most serious challenge yet to the South African Government's still controversial "outwards movement."

The whole future of the policy may be wrapped up in the way South Africa responds overtly and covertly to Chief Leabua Jonathan's decision to declare a state of emergency, suspend the Constitution, and arrest the leaders of the Opposition Congress Party.

One of the major objectives of the "outwards movement" is to prove to a sceptical world that "racialistic" South Africa is capable of living in peace with her Black neighbours; that she is capable of tolerating their non-racial policies; that she respects their sovereignty, and that she is capable of aiding them towards prosperity without robbing them of their independence.

Here Chief Leabua Jonathan's conservative pro-South African Government has been defeated at the polls (so far unofficially) by the more militant, more Socialistic and definitely anti-South African Congress Party which is widely believed to have strong links with Communist China.

The problems of co-existing with a Lesotho regime under Congress leader Ntsu Mokhehle would be tremendous.

By the same token, the temptation to covertly aid Chief Leabua Jonathan and thus perpetuate a regime that offers no problems in the realm of co-existence must be great.

However, if South Africa does yield to temptation and if she is caught at it, what credibility she has achieved in the world with the "outwards movement" would be destroyed.

1970

King Moshoeshoe being sworn in as the Queen's representative in Basutoland—shortly before the country became the independent state of Lesotho. "He has abdicated," said Chief Jonathan today.

Mr Ntsu Mokhehle, leader of the opposition Congress Party, who claims his party won the election and who, according to Chief Jonathan, is to be detained indefinitely.

Congress Party clear winners

The Star's Africa News Service

MASERU. — Now that the first shock waves of Chief Leabua Jonathan's emergency declaration are dying down, people are beginning to ask what went wrong for Chief Jonathan.

The official black-out of information is still in force but it is clear that Mr. Ntsu Mokhehle's Congress Party emerged from the election a clear winner by at least six seats.

This represents a significant swing in support from the National Party which has ruled Lesotho since responsible government was granted.

In the April, 1965, election, the Congress Party trailed the National Party by six seats and 5 000 votes, with four seats going to the pro-monarchist Marematlou Freedom Party.

The reasons for the shift are many and none too clear, but a growing sense of national identity has made many Sotho less satisfied with the country's relations with South Africa.

Chief Jonathan has been one of South Africa's few friends in Black Africa, mainly because Lesotho, being entirely surrounded by its apartheid neighbour and dependent upon her economically, has little choice in the matter.

EMOTIONAL

But Ntsu Mokhehle's promise of a harder line has great emotional appeal for many, and while the party leader is friendly and even charming with Europeans, many of his followers are anti-White.

Another factor in bringing the majority of the country behind the Congress Party may well be the patchy development.

Where development has taken place, there was a swing.

1970

"S.A. TOLD LEABUA: CONCEDE VICTORY"

By STANLEY UYS

CAPE TOWN, Saturday.

ON JANUARY 30 — the day on which Prime Minister Leabua Jonathan made his broadcast announcing the nullification of Lesotho's general election — he received a secret message "from the highest levels of the South African Government," says a report published in London in The Times today.

"The message said the South Africans had heard what the chief planned to do, expressed disapproval, and emphatically advised him to concede the election to the opposition."

This report was sent by the newspaper's Southern African staff correspondent, Mr. Dan van der Vat, who has just returned to Cape Town from a visit to Lesotho.

Jurists

The report also states: "On the afternoon of January 29, Chief Jonathan, as he himself said, consulted the two South African jurists who act as the two leading law officers in his administration, on the legal implications of declaring a state of emergency. They saw no obstacles, but apparently advised against suspending the constitution."

Having suspended the constitution, Chief Jonathan's problem now is how to "get off the hook", says Mr. Van der Vat. He has appointed a commission of inquiry into alleged electoral abuses, and the new constitution will be published next month and put to the people "by means of a sounding-out exercise rather than a referendum," and thereafter, if Chief Jonathan is satisfied that peace and stability have returned, he will "start thinking of a new election."

February 1970

I HAVE NOW SEIZED POWER SAYS JONATHAN

The Star's Africa News Service

Maseru.

CHIEF LEABUA JONATHAN, Prime Minister of Lesotho, openly admitted this afternoon that he had seized power in his country by suspending the constitution and declaring a state of emergency.

"I am not ashamed of it. It may appear to be undemocratic but I know my country and the majority of the people are behind me," he told more than 40 international journalists at a Press conference here.

Chief Jonathan said that the head of state, King Moshoeshoe II, had automatically abdicated by involving himself in the politics of the general election.

The arrested leader of the opposition Congress Party, Mr. Ntsu Mokhehle, would be detained indefinitely.

Free elections would be held under a new constitution but, even if the Congress Party won, he would not allow it to assume government unless he was satisfied that the elections were democratic.

BOXES SEIZED

The Prime Minister declared that he had proof that Congress Party supporters had seized ballot boxes after Tuesday's voting and that there had been many acts of violence before and during the balloting.

See "Years of trouble..."
—Page 3

He held his Press conference exactly 24 hours after his shock seizure of power in Lesotho, when there were strong indications that the Congress Party had won 33 of the 60 parliamentary seats and were, therefore, to take over government.

Asked if he considered the declaration of a state of emergency and the suspension of the constitution to be legal, he replied: "As far as I am concerned it is legal."

KING AGREED

He gave no details of what is likely to happen to the King. He denied that the King was under house arrest in his Maseru palace. The King was merely not permitted to communicate with anyone, without the prior approval of the Prime Minister.

"You can't interview the King of England."

Last Sunday, two days before voting day, the King had held a meeting at the royal village of Matsieng 25 miles from Maseru, Chief Jonathan said.

There the King had advised district chiefs and headmen to get their people to back the Congress Party.

LAND THREAT

Many supporters of the National Party — led by Chief Jonathan — were threatened with the loss of their land if they voted, said Chief Jonathan.

He did not intend to release to the public the final results of the election because it had been declared invalid. But he admitted that there had been a swing of voters to the Congress Party.

"This swing was because of violence and intimidation. A swing of 60 per cent could never have happened here. It has never happened in Britain or America or anywhere else."

Asked why he waited until most of the results were known before declaring the state of emergency, Chief Jonathan said he had to wait until he received sufficient information about violent incidents.

He was not able to say when new elections would be held. They would not take place until thuggery had disappeared and people could vote freely.

"If the Congress Party should win the election then, I will hand over power, provided I am satisfied that things had been done democratically."

He confirmed that about 15 Congress Party leaders had been arrested. "There will be many more. We are rounding up the troublemakers."

NOT REPUBLICAN

Despite his statement that the King had automatically abdicated, Chief Jonathan said he did not think that Lesotho's new constitution would be a republican one.

"We are dedicated to the concept of a constitutional monarchy."

The new constitution would be drafted by the government's constitutional lawyers but all groups would be consulted, including the opposition.

The Chief Justice, Mr. Justice H. R. Jacobs, a South African, would not take part in the drafting.

January 1970

King Moshoeshoe II of Lesotho and the Prime Minister, Chief Leabua Jonathan, had a friendly talk at a cocktail party last week.

Jonathan and his King bury old spears

By CAREL BIRKBY

CHIEF LEABUA JONATHAN, the tough Prime Minister of Lesotho, and King Moshoeshoe II have made peace. At a cocktail party last week I saw Chief Jonathan raise his glass and propose a formal toast to "His Majesty." Afterwards the Prime Minister told me that he and the King were friends again — old spears were buried.

The Prime Minister said: "It is clearly understood that the King is a constitutional monarch. His status is similar to that of Queen Elizabeth of England. Queen Elizabeth would not interfere in political affairs. Nor will the King.

"As friends we both realise that Lesotho can only progress in a condition of political stability. That is being achieved, and we are friends."

The King, now returned from exile, smiled his agreement.

The two men are obviously on good terms after years of tension.

They first clashed soon after Independence Day more than four years ago. The King maintained a liaison with the Opposition groups, and a consequence of the unrest that followed the riot at Thaba Bosiu, the heartland of the Basotho nation, which led to the killing of ten people.

Confined

The Prime Minister imposed palace arrest on the King. Nobody could see him unless the Government gave permission — and that was rarely.

He was forced to sign an oath undertaking not to take part in politics — on pain of self-agreed abdication.

Then the King was removed from the scene, while a state of emergency prevailed in the country, by a visit, diplomatically arranged, to Holland to "continue his studies."

The Oxford-educated King, a quiet, studious man, spent the best part of a year in The Hague. In December he was allowed back to his homeland. The restrictions on him have been lifted. He is no longer confined to his palace in Maseru. He spends a lot of time at the Royal village of Matsieng. His younger brother, who under the emergency regulations was restricted to Mokhotlong, a remote village in the Mont-aux-Sources peaks, is now allowed to come to Maseru to visit him.

The King drives around freely, plays games of squash at the Maseru Club, usually with old friends among the British community, and sees the latest movies screened in the new Holiday Inn.

But until a few weeks ago the people had not seen him in company with the Prime Minister. Then Chief Jonathan sent his own car to the palace, inviting the King to attend a football match with him. The people saw them together and cheered.

The conciliation was seen to be complete when at last week's cocktail party they shook hands and talked amicably and vivaciously together.

1970-71

The newspaper cutting below, written in the days immediately after the coup, appeared in *The Star*, based in Johannesburg. I am including it but I do question the veracity of some of the information, which is alarmist in the extreme and although elements of it could have been true, I believe that the overall picture of tensions and BCP threat of violent anti-government activities built up by this article is very overblown.

MASERU, Saturday.

CHIEF LEABUA JONATHAN'S Government, which three weeks ago seized power unconstitutionally after discovering, at the last minute, an Opposition plot to take over control in the country, is sitting on a powder keg which may explode soon unless he takes swift and strong action.

Although the words "Kena Ka Khotso" (Enter in Peace) welcome the visitor to the Maseru border post, the present "peace and calm" seem to be superficial, as there are strong undercurrents of tension, uncertainty and fear.

This state of affairs is best illustrated by the chaotic events on Thursday night when it was reported that there was a Congress Party attack on the Maseru police station.

What happened was that a platoon of the Police Mobile Unit went into an African township to look for Mr. K. Chakela, secretary ... of the Congress Party, who has been in hiding for two weeks. Fighting broke out between the platoon and party sympathisers.

Back in quiet Maseru, the central police station heard gunfire, sounded off their siren and fired flares in the air.

As police reinforcements were rushing into town the police were shooting at each other in the confusion, and one was killed.

Early action

This incident has shown how a small, well organised Congress Party gang could exploit the uncertainty to cause general confusion.

For Chief Jonathan to retain control and stay in power, he must, in the next two weeks, do the following:

● Immediately arrest the Peking-trained Congress Party ringleaders who were mistakenly not arrested at the outset.

● Confiscate large supplies of hidden arms and raid the secret backyard "factories"

where hand weapons and bombs are being manufactured.

● Take firm action against an unknown number of military trained Opposition gangs who are spread in secret camps throughout the country, some of whom have been kidnapping and killing Jonathan supporters.

● Consolidate his position in the Civil Service — with 80 per cent pro-BCP supporters — and in the police force, where the loyalty of certain officers and men is suspect.

There are signs that the Jonathan Government has underestimated the seriousness of the situation. There is a surprising lack of urgency in their counter-measures in view of the alarming nature of some of the information at their disposal.

At present, Congress Party tactics are undecided. A spokesman told me: "We are scared of an uprising as long as our leaders are in jail. But once Mokhehle is free, we will never accept a Jonathan dictatorship but will fight to the last man."

The next few weeks are vital as Congress Party action will be determined by what is decided on the future of the King Mokhehle, a new constitution and whether if ever, there will be new elections.

Whites threatened in Lesotho

SUNDAY TIMES REPORTER

MASERU, Saturday.

EVIDENCE that a secret anti-White campaign has been mounted against certain permanent White residents of Lesotho by militant elements of the Congress Party has come to light in Maseru.

As the Whites concerned are too scared to talk about it openly, very little is heard about this new development in Lesotho.

A White citizen and his wife who have lived in Lesotho for most of their lives spoke to me today on the South African side of the border, out of fear of retaliation against them.

This man told me: "A few days ago a group of three Congress Party supporters approached my house at night and tried to force details out of my Lesotho servant about the room in which I slept. My servant was told that either he or I would be killed if he refused to tell them.

"The servant, however, assured them that he did not know anything. They then warned him that if he spoke about the incident to me his whole family would suffer.

"Immediately after they had left he told me what had happened. The police were informed, but the gang could not be found."

The Star, Johannesburg, February 1970

Freddy Roach, Strong Man Behind the Coup

If one studies the transition from colonial rule to independence and events of insurrection in subsequent years, it frequently involves a former police or army officer, sometimes black and sometimes white: For example, Idi Amin in Uganda or Colonel Mike Hoare in the Seychelle Islands, among others. In Lesotho, Freddy Roach, promoted to Police Commissioner and for three years developmental officer for Lesotho's tough paramilitary contingent, was crucial to the bloodless success of Chief Leabua's January 1970 coup.

Chief Leabua knew that he enjoyed the absolute loyalty of Freddy Roach and in turn the paramilitary contingent. And the opposition knew that Freddy Roach and his men would deal severely with any disturbances. I believe I am on safe ground in saying that "strong man" Freddy Roach in the wings was central to Chief Leabua having the confidence to stage a coup.

The first picture taken for publication of Lesotho's "strongman," Mr. Freddy Roach, with his family at their guarded home in Maseru. With Mr. Roach is his vivacious wife, Patricia, and their children (from left), Jennifer, 8, Alison, 7, and Teresa, 11.

Mixing with Royalty
Meeting Princess Marina

In October 1966, Princess Marina represented the Queen at the Lesotho Independence Celebrations. Because I was Director of the celebrations I had a lot of personal contact with Princess Marina and her Secretary, Sir Philip Hay, during the four days that they were in Lesotho. She was a very dignified, charming lady and I got on well with her and with Sir Philip as well. On Princess Marina's last night in Lesotho, Sir Philip paid me the compliment of electing to take the night off and entrusted Princess Marina to my sole care. We attended a concert which was part of the official program.

On her departure from Lesotho she presented me with a pair of gold cufflinks embossed with the Kent coat of arms. The fact that the celebrations were successful and passed without any hitches helped establish such a good relationship. Tracy was born two weeks after the celebrations and we received a telegram of congratulations from Princess Marina.

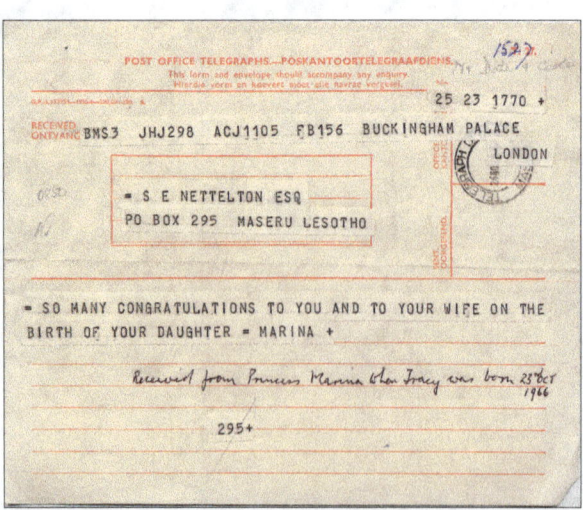

Telegram from Princess Marina received by Gail and I after the birth of Tracy.

Tea at Wimbledon

The following year when Gail and I were in the UK, Sir Philip contacted me and arranged tickets for us to attend Wimbledon. In the afternoon at Wimbledon we were invited to tea in the royal enclosure. Princess Marina greeted us personally then handed us over to be chaperoned by her lady in waiting. There we were sipping our tea with Princess Margaret and Harold MacMillan (former British Prime Minister) and many other dignitaries.

Princess Marina tragically died of a stroke a few years later. She would have been a great loss to the Royal family. On that same visit we attended an investiture at Buckingham Place presided over by the Queen where I received an MBE.

Outside Buckingham Palace after the investiture, 1965.

All the world's a stage

Written by William Shakespeare (1559 or early 1600, first published in the folio of 1623). This summation of a person's life written so long ago is as true today as it was in the 17th century—and it applies equally well in every country of the world. I believe, as I write, that I am in the sixth stage of my life with one to go. Shakespeare's 'Seven Stages of Man' from 'As You Like It' is reproduced here.

All the world's a stage,
And all the men and women merely players;
They have their exits and their entrances;
And one man in his time plays many parts;
His acts being seven ages. At first, the infant,
Mewling and puking in the nurse's arms;
Then the whining schoolboy, with his satchel
And shining morning face, creeping like snail
Unwillingly to school. And then the lover,
Sighing like furnace, with a woeful ballad
Made to his mistress' eyebrow. Then a soldier,
Full of strange oaths and bearded like the pard,
Jealous in honor, sudden and quick in quarrel,
Seeking the bubble reputation
Even in the cannon's mouth. And then the justice,
In fair round belly with good capon lin'd,
With eyes severe and beard of formal cut,
Full of wise saws and modern instances;
And so he plays his part. The sixth age shifts
Into the lean and slipper'd pantaloon,
With spectacles on nose and pouch on side;
His youthful hose, well sav'd, a world too wide
For his shrunk shank; and his big manly voice,

Turning again toward childish treble, pipes
And whistles in his sound. Last scene of all,
That ends this strange eventful history,
Is second childishness and mere oblivion;
Sans teeth, sans eyes, sans taste, sans everything.

In the remote Lesotho mountains the seven stages are played out as they are everywhere else in the world. *Seeking the bubble reputation / Even in the cannon's mouth:* The young men in remote villages tear all over the place on their horses where the young teenage girls hoeing the wheat fields can see them. In the city the same age young men tear around in their souped-up cars. The motive for these young men whether in far away mountains or in the highly populated streets of the city is the same: to impress the girls — sex! And the need for excitement. Many young men go to war because they crave adventure, excitement, danger.

Shakespeare was a remarkable man in his grasp of the human character.

Young lads on their horses—no different from more affluent societies where the young lads race around in their cars.

Family Tragedies

Over the years every family has its tragedies and we can claim our share. The fact that our family frequently travelled abroad "in service of the Crown" exposed us to danger; on other occasions the adventurous spirit which seems to be part of our make-up had fatal consequences. I have pieced together the tragedies that I am aware of.

Gerald Clement Nettelton (1930-1958)

My elder brother. Killed when elephant shooting near Dodoma in Tanzania. Gerald was a District Officer in the British Colonial service stationed at Dodoma. He was a very cheerful, well-liked person who shot elephants for sport and also to make a bit of extra money by selling the ivory. He was trampled to death by his twenty-fifth elephant. He wounded the elephant and very foolishly followed it into thick bush. The elephant ambushed him and trampled him to death. His tracker said it had the best pair of tusks he had ever seen. The wounded elephant was never found.

Left and right: My brother, Gerald Clement Nettelton

Robert Eales (1921-1968)

My first cousin. Killed in a motorcycle accident in the Eastern Cape, South Africa. Robert was an architect. He loved his motorcycle, which he often rode to work.

Peter Ellenberger (1924-1956)

My first cousin. Killed in a motor accident in Rhodesia, aged thirty-two. He was an officer in the Rhodesian Department of Native Affairs and had survived three years active service in North Africa and Italy during the Second World War, 1939-45. He was not married.

David Enraght Moony (1866-1896)

My great-uncle. Younger brother of Grandmother Nettelton. Killed in Rhodesia in 1897 during the Mashona Rebellion. He was a magistrate at the time. The full story is in another volume of my memoirs.

Sir Spencer Perceval

Spencer Perceval was a British Foreign Minister in the Pitt Government and became Prime Minister in 1804. Murdered in the foyer of the British House of Commons in 1806. My great-grandfather, Sir Charles Cherry Minchin, married a Perceval in direct line of descent from Sir Spencer Perceval. That story is also in another volume of my memoirs.

Queen's Birthday Honours Disappointment

In 1967, I was awarded an MBE. To this day my MBE remains in my bottom drawer, unloved.

Prior to the official announcement of the awards, I had been advised by both the British High Commissioner in Lesotho and the Government Secretary that I was to be awarded an OBE (Officer of the British Empire) for my work as both District Commissioner, Mokhotlong and Director of the Independence Celebrations. After being told the above about my award, the "powers that be" in Whitehall said that Lesotho was already awarding three OBEs to local Basotho recipients and so my award had to be delayed to a later appropriate time. And there the matter sat for over a year. I could have broached the matter a hundred times with the Prime Minister but I never did. The matter was eventually dealt with but I received an MBE not an OBE. A colleague who I asked to chase up the matter got an OBE. The circumstances are an issue best left alone. I can assure my family that it was in no way the result of any misdemeanour on my part and that the matter is now long forgotten with no feelings of resentment. Anyway, it was fun to go to Buckingham Palace and have a gong pinned to my breast by the Queen in person, even if it was only an MBE.

When I left Lesotho, the Prime Minister threw a big farewell party for me attended by the full Cabinet and all Heads of Department and other dignitaries and presented me with a mohair rug. A few years later when on holidays in South Africa, in 1980, I called on Leabua and he presented me with a beautiful mohair shawl. For quite a few years after I left Lesotho we periodically exchanged letters, with his relative, Mosito Molapo, acting as his scribe. These letters are not for publication.

Departure for Australia November 1969 and a Voyage on the Himalaya

In July 1969 we left Basutoland. It was the right time to go. Pressure to Africanise senior government positions was intense. I had seen a number of my European colleagues endeavour to hang on, only to fall foul of an African Minister with the result that they departed full of bitterness because of their last three months, and the previous fifteen good and happy years were forgotten. We didn't want this to happen to us. We were still on the crest of the wave and that's the way it was when we drove out of Maseru, Basutoland, for the last time with Australia our chosen destination.

We had no problems being accepted as Australian immigrants. Those were the days of the £10 passage and we were as a family readily approved. We had come to know the Australian High Commissioner in South Africa quite well. When he visited Basutoland we saw him socially and I took him out trout fishing a couple of times. On one occasion four of us flew up to Semongkong where the trout fishing was quite good and we stayed overnight at a very basic rest house. The plane was weighed down by cartons of beer. We arrived at Semongkong at breakfast time and the High Commissioner and his Australian colleague wasted no time getting stuck into the beer in true Aussie style. The Aussie contingent caught no trout, never looked like catching any. Fortunately Desmond and I were quite successful so we dined well on trout that night and, you guessed it, lots of beer!

At the time I left Basutoland I enjoyed Permanent Secretary level which in modern terms would be CEO to a Government department. I was offered a position with the World Food Program of the United Nations to be positioned in Botswana, but refused after much soul searching. The WFP were very keen to get me, and Gail and I had spent a day with Eric Robinson, head of the WFP, when we visited Rome in 1967. Eric had kept in touch with me even after our departure for Australia and continued to assure me that the offer remained open. He consistently stated that he wanted me to do one three-year tour in the field and then join him in the WFP headquarters in Rome. In 1972, two years after we had settled in Adelaide, there was a firm offer to look after the WFP affairs in Fiji. I came within a whisker of accepting! If we had indeed taken up the offer our lives would have taken a very different course.

After leaving Basutoland that July day we took it very easy for the next four months visiting friends and relations. Bevie and Tracy were four and three years old respectively so there were no schooling complications, and adoring grannies and grandpas received us warmly. I had received a generous golden handshake from the British Government so there were no money issues to consider — and our fourteen-day voyage from Durban to Sydney (with time spent in Perth, Adelaide and Melbourne along the way) had set us back £40 for the whole family.

Eventually the date of departure arrived. Gail's parents and a few others came to see us off. Mark and Pat Chapman very kindly came all the way from Basutoland. Gail's parents by this stage were themselves planning to emigrate to Australia, which they did three years later, so the departure was not painful for them.

Arriving at the dock.

The voyage was pretty routine. Gail and I had each done five return voyages from Cape Town to the UK (ten days each way) so we were very familiar with life on the high seas. From the early 1970s immigrants to Australia were brought out increasingly by air rather than sea.

Our day in Perth was hot and dry. Three days later Adelaide was even hotter. I well remember looking out of the porthole on arrival in Adelaide and there in front of us was the old corrugated iron reception shed for immigrants at Outer Harbour. A nice building was built about the time the last immigrant boat arrived—good planning! We took a bus trip into Adelaide. We were impressed by Veale Gardens where the roses were beautiful but there was a hot northerly wind blowing and it was dusty and not very welcoming—Adelaide was not for us! Six months later when we revisited, the rains had been good, everything was green and lush and we loved the architecture. We bought a house and stayed!

The old "Himalaya" steamed on to Melbourne where we spent a day and then we disembarked at Sydney where Tony and Flea Turner met us. We spent two weeks with them which was a great introduction to Australia and then off we went in a Sunderland flying boat to Lord Howe Island for three and a half months.